Deco & Streamline Architecture in L.A.

A Moderne City Survey

Elizabeth McMillian

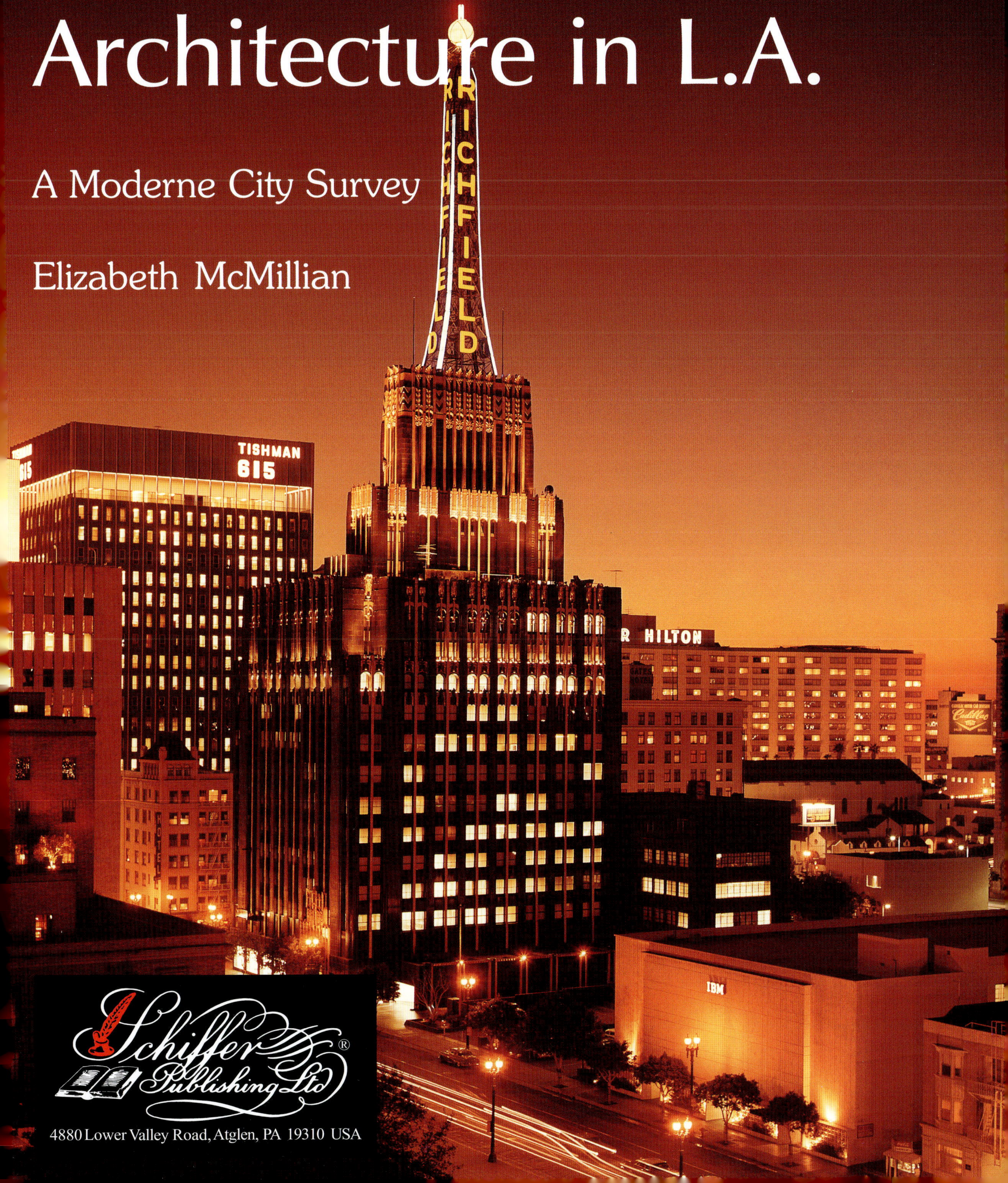

Schiffer Publishing Ltd®
4880 Lower Valley Road, Atglen, PA 19310 USA

Title page:
Likely L.A.'s best example of the Art Deco phase of the Moderne Style, the 1928 Richfield Building was a dramatic towering structure sheathed in black terra-cotta with gilded trim. Its upper stories were a series of setbacks crowned by a 120-foot steel-trussed tower, which carried the sign for the building and was lit in neon at night. Now demolished, it was designed by Stiles O. Clements with the firm Morgan Walls & Clements. *Tom Zimmerman*

Opposite page:
The Smith House, 1929-30, designed by J. Clarence Smale, is a rare example of a single-family Art Deco residence. It is located in the Hancock Park area. *Elizabeth McMillian*

Library of Congress Cataloging-in-Publication Data

McMillian, Elizabeth Jean.
Deco & streamline architecture in L.A. / by Elizabeth McMillian.
p. cm.
ISBN 0-7643-2008-4 (hardcover)
1. Architecture--California--Los Angeles-20th century. 2. Art deco (Architecture)--California--Los Angeles. 3. Los Angeles (Calif.)--Buildings, structures, etc. I. Title: Deco and streamline architecture in L.A. II. Title.
NA735.L55 M38 2004
720'.9794'9409041--dc22
2003023931

Designed by Ellen J. "Sue" Taltoan
Type set in Zapf Humanist Dm BT/Souvenir Lt BT

ISBN: 0-7643-2008-4
Printed in China

Published by Schiffer Publishing Ltd.
4880 Lower Valley Road
Atglen, PA 19310
Phone: (610) 593-1777; Fax: (610) 593-2002
E-mail: Info@schifferbooks.com

For the largest selection of fine reference books on this and related subjects, please visit our web site at
www.schifferbooks.com
We are always looking for people to write books on new and related subjects. If you have an idea for a book please contact us at the above address.

This book may be purchased from the publisher.
Include $3.95 for shipping.
Please try your bookstore first.
You may write for a free catalog.

In Europe, Schiffer books are distributed by
Bushwood Books
6 Marksbury Ave.
Kew Gardens
Surrey TW9 4JF England
Phone: 44 (0) 20 8392-8585; Fax: 44 (0) 20 8392-9876
E-mail: info@bushwoodbooks.co.uk
Free postage in the U.K., Europe; air mail at cost.

Contents

Acknowledgments 4
Preface 5
Defining Terms For a Style and Its Two Main Phases 5

Introduction 7
From Art Nouveau To Avant-Garde: Mutual Sources For The Moderne and The Modern Movement 7
The International Influence of The Avant-Garde Modern Movement 13
From Ballets Russes To Modern Jazz: Moderne Distinctions 15
From Art Deco Tower To Streamline Slab: Moderne In America 24

I. L.A.'s Deco and Streamline Styles In Context 36
A Socio-Political Note 36
The Fine Line Between Modern and Moderne 40
Moderne Structuring of Architecture and Industrial Design 53
Furnishings and Art For The Moderne Style 59

II. Deco Details and Streamline Structure 62
Art Deco Elements 62
Streamline Elements 80

III. A Moderne City Survey 89
Art Deco Style 89
Streamline Style 141
PWA and Classical Moderne 172
Regency Moderne 198
L.A.'s Moderne Legacy 205

Endnotes 235
Resources by Bettye Young 236
Bibliography 239

Acknowledgments

I wish to thank photographers Tom Zimmerman, Renee Hadar, Tim Street-Porter, David Glomb, Jason Schmidt, Benny Chan, and Gene Ogami for use of their photographs, and the L.A. Conservancy and the Deco Society for their information and advocacy in saving Los Angeles' Deco and Streamline works. Residents Jules Hammovitz, Adele Yellin, Tom and Nancy Michali, Peter and Julie Pascal, Beatrice and Chap Findlay kindly opened their houses for photography, as did the Garfield Building's owners Yoav and Botach Shlomo. Marmol Radziner and Associates, and Kelly Wearstler of *kwid* provided photos and information about their contemporary Moderne-inspired designs. For their assistance, I also thank interior designer Carolyn M. Lawrence, French decorative arts dealer Anne Hauck, collector/arts dealer James Marrin, architectural historian Leslie Heumann, architect/historian John Chase, and particularly my copy editor Melissa Brandzel, publishers Nancy and Peter Schiffer, and B. Jordan Young for her invaluable resources.

A large community hall with all the characteristics of a 1932-33 Chicago World's Fair building, the green-stuccoed 1938 Pan-Pacific Auditorium featured its Streamline decoration – four fin-shaped pylons with repetitive banding over its entrance. This fine example of L.A.'s Streamline Moderne was damaged by fire in May 1989, yet the original entrance was rebuilt later to accommodate a new community center at 7600 Beverly Boulevard. The original structure was the design of Walter Wurdeman and Weldon Becket; the restoration and new construction were by architect Jeffrey Kalban. *Tim Street-Porter*

Preface

Los Angeles' Art Deco styles fall into two main categories: the zigzag, perpendicular Deco style of the 1920s and the aerodynamic, cubist style of the Streamline 1930s and early '40s. Allied with these are the many L.A. works that are called PWA and Classical Moderne of the 1920s and '30s, and the playful Regency Moderne of the late '30s and '40s. All celebrate a populist, progressive, machine-age city. This analysis draws comparison with the Modern Movement to reveal similar roots and the pragmatic, mechanistic differences that led America – and Los Angeles, in particular – to produce a wealth of buildings in these exuberant styles.

Given its unlikely combination of sunshine, European émigrés, film-making, and consumerist culture, L.A. faced the Great Depression by quickly modifying its attitude toward the rich materials and decorative forms of the Deco '20s era. By doing so, the city was able to accommodate the economic reserve of the '30s and '40s – and simultaneously offer the pizzazz of the nation's 1933 and '39 World Fairs and the new prominence of industrial design.

The rich angular ornament, towers, graphics, and exaggerated representation of structure (in terms of multiple linear mouldings, exterior banding and curves, and unnecessary interior soffits, for example) offered decorative representations of technical and industrial process and gave mechanistic purpose to a beneficial capitalist L.A. Its architects and designers of the 1920s to 1940s processed and integrated European Modern Movement theories and architectural expressions in a manner that suited L.A.'s own special culture.

Defining Terms For a Style and Its Two Main Phases

Many people generalize and equate the terms **Moderne** and **Art Deco**.[1] While this lack of distinction is fine in the popular culture which promoted its vernacular growth, local historians immediately foresaw the difficulties. As my mentors, David Gebhard and Robert Winter, noted in 1977:

> Though the term Art Deco has recently been employed to describe the Moderne, it is not satisfactory, since it does not take into account the diversity of sources, nor does it mirror the major difference between the Moderne of the '20s and the Moderne of the '30s.[2]

Recognizing the same dissatisfaction, I find the term Art Deco, or simply Deco, a more appropriate description of the first phase than **Zigzag Moderne** (also referred to as the **Perpendicular Style**), since the Art Deco label reflects the highly decorative aspects of the style and respects its roots in French Modernism. In this analysis of the spirited decorative modernism that arose in Los Angeles architecture and design of the 1920s and 1930s, I prefer to use the French word **Moderne** as an umbrella term covering both the **Art Deco** and **Streamline** styles.

In the glossary of Gebhard and Winter's first regional guidebook, *A Guide to Architecture in Southern California*, they defined the Moderne Style by first dividing it into two different phases: the Zigzag Moderne of the 1920s (which I call the Art Deco phase) and the Streamline Moderne of the 1930s. They wrote:

> The Zigzag Moderne [of the 1920s] developed from classical-inspired designs of the teens and early '20s by Bertram B. Goodhue and from the vertical Gothic schemes of Eliel Saarinen, from the forms and ornamentation of the Paris Exposition des Arts Décoratif of 1925, as well as the teens and '20s designs of Frank Lloyd Wright. A final influence was the then-newly developing International Style.
>
> The Streamline Moderne [of the 1930s] was an outgrowth of the machine aesthetic, the curved aerodynamic form of the airplane and of an even more intensified influence of the International Style.[3]

Today, the use of the French term Moderne distinguishes the populist movement from the theoretically-based Modern Movement. While their straight lines and simplified forms appear related, the Moderne seemed to be a part of, and coexisted with, other styles of the international Modern Movement, which are variously called Bauhaus, Rationalism, De Stijl, International Style and more. However, many of the Moderne's buildings reflected traditional classical styles reduced to produce a sense of Modern*ism*, which was yet another label bandied about as loosely in the 1920s and '30s as it is today, implying the same derivative character due to a dependence on the true innovation and recognized character of the Modern Movement.

The Streamline Taylor House, 1935, by Milton J. Black, located in the Los Feliz area. *Elizabeth McMillian*

Introduction

From Art Nouveau To Avant-Garde: Mutual Sources For The Moderne and The Modern Movement

The elements of the Moderne – like those of the Modern Movement – had their roots in the turn of the twentieth century and its early years. The style came into existence with the influence of Russian ballet design for sets, costumes, and graphics, and thrived under the total architecture-to-furnishings interests of Art Nouveau (also called Jugendstil, Modern Style, Viennese Secessionist, and Liberty). In France, architects who influenced the Moderne included Auguste Perret and Charles Garnier; in England, William Morris; in Belgium, Victor Horta and Henry van de Velde; in Scotland, Charles Rennie Mackintosh; and in Austria, Otto Wagner, Josef Hoffmann, Joseph Maria Olbrich, and Adolf Loos.

The importance of Art Nouveau to both the Moderne Style and the Modern Movement lies in an emerging new perception of architecture and design. This break from tradition was clearly stated by van de Velde, who wrote in his autobiography:

> The brief interlude of art nouveau, that ephemeral will o'the wisp which knew no other law than its own caprice, was succeeded, as I had foretold, by the hesitant beginnings of a new, a disciplined and purposeful style, the style of our own age. Two world wars have prolonged its growing pains. But step by step it pursues its conscious advance towards maturity. And that maturity, when finally attained, will synchronize with the realization of a rationalized aesthetic, whereby beauty of form can be immunized against current infections from the noisome parasite fantasy.[4]

The 1913 Springman House at Hagen by Belgian architect, Henry Van de Velde. *K.E. Osthaus, van de Velde, 1920*

Otto Wagner's drawing for a Viennese Housing Block, 1911. *J.A. Lux, Otto Wagner, 1914*

The term *nouveau* expressed the rejection of traditional styles and construction on which European architecture had been based. The revolt against tradition was the most important common characteristic of the various European trends, although it was a purely negative one. While many criticized the preciousness of the movement (such as Walter Crane, who called it a "decorative illness"[5]), in Glasgow, a group of artists and Mackintosh began a new interpretation of Art Nouveau in which the linear arabesques of Beardsley-type decoration led to a means of defining *spatial* characteristics as square, and solid wood or metal elements interacted with curved and imaginative ornament. These characteristics were exhibited in Mackintosh's furniture at the Vienna Secession in 1900 and at the international exhibit in Turin in 1902. In conception, Mackintosh was actually closer to the Medievalism of John Ruskin and William Morris, and by the first decade of the twentieth century, Mackintosh's heritage, like that of Morris' social ideals, passed to the *avant-garde* continental movements.

The experiments of French architects Auguste Perret and Tony Garnier also contributed to the forming of the Modern Movement in the first decade of the twentieth century. However, through these architects, France actually participated in the international Modern Movement while staying within its traditional lines. Since French culture was thoroughly based on Classicism as well as refined technical traditions, Perret and Garnier broadened the tenets of Classicism by freeing it from academic rules and using it to meet modern needs. Their works revolted against eclecticism while holding to the principles of Classicism – as geometry and clarity, as well as structural coherence – as produced through the new material and technical process of reinforced concrete.

> [Perret's] particular merit was to have sensed that this glorious tradition, impoverished by eclecticism, still had a margin of unexplored possibilities to help resolve the problem of our time, and to have developed these possibilities courageously.... With Perret the last cycle of French academic culture was concluded, with incomparable dignity, once and for all.[6]

Scottish architect Charles Rennie Mackintosh's drawing for a teahouse in Glasgow, circa 1905. *Sheldon Cheney, The New World Architecture, 1930*

Palais Stoclet, Brussels, 1905-11, designed by Austrian architect Josef Hoffmann. *ACL, Brussels*

Tony Garnier added to Perret's development the idea that one could find some harmony between traditions and produce works for a modern life accepting of social and scientific progress. His favorite study was of an industrial city built with reinforced concrete, iron, and glass that allowed for vital hygienic factors, such as sun, air and vegetation, as well as providing pedestrian and motor routes among well-spaced buildings. He had the opportunity to build his Utopian ideal at Lyon between 1904 and 1914, bridging theory and practice.

In Austria, Otto Wagner's Art Nouveau or Viennese Secessionist interpretation was similar to that of Mackintosh, Perret, and Garnier. He felt that architecture should free itself from imitations of the past and take modern technical conditions into account. Wagner taught that the whole of architecture could be liberated by this method and that even traditional elements could become adaptable to new needs. His approach was rich in consequences and was to become one of the basic components of European *avant-garde* taste, even when the Modern Movement had eliminated the references to historical styles. It was linked to the neo-Classical repertoire which provided the measure of comparison for every new element – as well as eventually relating it to the Moderne.

While Wagner and other Austrians were involved in modernist controversies, Loos was traveling in England and America from 1893 to 1896. After he returned to Vienna, he became active as a theorist from 1903 on and his theories distinguish him from his contemporaries. "One may do something new only if one is going to do it better. Only the inventions – electric light, concrete, etc.…can change tradition," he wrote.[7] Loos finally arrived at a complete separation of art and utility, placing architecture in the sphere of utility alone: "Architecture is not an art…[A]nything that fulfills a purpose is excluded from the sphere of art."[8]

Loos' "Ornament and Crime" article, 1908, went further to claim that architecture and the industrial arts should eliminate all ornament and that any decoration should be considered as a survival of unnecessary past customs. While one might think his distinction from his contemporaries perhaps was influenced by his American and British travels, his free use of space in the vertical sense was found not in American *avant-garde,* but in its current domestic building, which he felt followed objective demands of function.

Richard Neutra, a pupil of Loos, related how Loos worked from a "human measure of space"[9] instead of the wasteful practice of academic architects who filled up space and structure with ornament. Loos recognized the space where human activities took place as a practical reality that must be respected and not trivialized. Examples such as Loos' Steiner House and his design of a house on Michaelerplatz were devoid of ornament and expressed his argument of beauty versus utility. However, in a very short time,

The Ruhlmann Pavilion at the Exposition Internationale des Arts Décoratif et Industriel Moderne, Paris, 1925, designed by Pierre Patout. *Sheldon Cheney, The New World Architecture, 1930*

the Modern Movement would question these terms and the simplicity of Loos' architecture that effectually derived from Wagner's process of simplification of the traditional repertoire. "Ultimately a simple theory like Loos' became an irrelevance."[10]

Finally, Art Nouveau and the Viennese Secession did not lead to any appreciable change in productive organization in the field of architecture and the applied arts. The prejudice of the reformers against mechanical processes frequently replaced an idealistic assessment of industrial values and thus turned on itself only to assert the formal representation of technical and industrial processes.

The Industrial Age and its artistic changes in Western society led to the pursuit of *avant-garde* culture from which these movements initiated. Out of Europe, *avant-garde* changes first appeared in the arts between 1905 and 1914, with advances in perspective and the entire concept of art when Cubism emerged. And in the sciences, between the same dates, Einstein proposed his theory of relativity, the hypothesis of quantum element of action (1905) and his atomic theory (1913). Certainly an *avant-garde* architectural and design theory would mean a change of conception, and far more than an Art Nouveau change of stylistic forms even if it were as radical as Loos' total denial of ornament.

Indeed, in Germany, via Walter Gropius and the Bauhaus School, the legacy of the *avant-garde* led to such a change and the basis of the Modern Movement. Gropius' point of view was that beauty and utility should be reconciled and that reasoning man in an industrial age provided the true value of things. Traditionalists looked to the past and sought true value in nature with its imitations in ornament and structural expression. Gropius and the whole of the Modern Movement did not provide ready-made solutions like the imitations of traditional styles, but offered *methodical* suggestions for various solutions in varying degrees.

Germany and Austria found the most favorable environment for the Modern Movement. Although the movement was a minority, between 1922 and 1931 it seemed to become a close-knit body as the same conceptions were spreading throughout Europe and overcoming national differences. Gropius' teachings were validated by developments outside the Bauhaus as he invited the best architects from various countries to seek a rationale for their modern experiments that went beyond their heritage. Through this common intent, the new *avant-garde* architectural culture emerged.

With World War I, the European *avant-garde* confronted political changes that reflected cultural progress. The progressive elite had come of age and were called upon to become the ruling class while the ensuing economic depression and inflation forced old classes to mix with one another, destroying the old social hierarchy and favoring innovation. Gropius realized the collective work he had begun at the Bauhaus in 1919 could hardly be in harmony with the aims of the political parties in Weimar Germany, as a profound political upheaval was growing which led Germany and many other European countries to dictatorships, and then to World War II. Modern architecture faced the conflict between democracy and dictatorship which emerged between 1930 and 1940. Architects of the Modern Movement confronted the authoritarian regimes and, because of the nature of the movement, the problem of the new architecture could not be reduced to a question of principle, but had to take practical shape as compromises and partial experiments.

L'Esprit Nouveau pavilion at the Exposition Internationale des Arts Décoratif et Industriel Moderne, Paris, 1925, designed by Le Corbusier (Charles-Edouard Jeanneret). *Museum of Modern Art*

In Germany, Gropius, Ludwig Mies van der Rohe, and others had been fostering State relations for some time. The Werkbund and the Bauhaus were State institutions, and the Dessau building and the Stuttgart Weissenhof had been paid for by public money. Gropius and his colleagues had resolved to make the State the means by which to translate their ideas into action. The Dutch had a similar experience, for they had been working through public administration for thirty years. Gropius and Dutch architects J.J.P. Oud and Hendrik Berlage knew that to work with the State meant giving up their privileged position of *avant-garde* artists, but they were willing to accept political struggle on an equal footing with their other countrymen. They put forward their proposals according to current rules, valid for all, and accepted the rules by asking for help from the State. If the response was democratic, there was some progress, and if it was totalitarian, modern architecture was passed over for powerful images of arches and columns.

In 1927, both the competition for the League of Nations and the Stuttgart exhibition showed the world that numerous European architects were working with similar methods and ideas and, in 1928, many of these architects felt it was time to form an association based on this unity in view of political changes. A supporter, Mme. de Mandrot, offered her castle at La Sarraz for this first congress of modern architects. The talk was optimistic in tone, while the problems of State support for modern architecture were of current interest and the participants were aware of the gravity of the problems. The name Congrès Internationaux d'Architecture Moderne (CIAM) was adopted, with an agreement to meet periodically for the purpose of comparing various experiments and deciding how to present the public with solutions.

In this flexible, informal manner, CIAM held together while individual European dispersion abounded. In 1932, the Nazis came to power at Dessau and the Bauhaus had to move to Berlin. Then, in 1933, when Hitler became Chancellor, Mies van der Rohe had to close the school down altogether. Between 1933 and 1938, Bauhaus teachers fled to America, England, Austria, and Russia. Nonetheless, by the time of the fourth congress of CIAM in 1941, the collective goals of the Modern Movement architects were published as the *Charte d'Athenes,* in which private interest would be subordinated to public interest in an attempt to produce an architecture and a city type that would work for everyone. The *avant-garde* of the Modern Movement had succeeded in producing an architectural theory and practice based on method rather than style, with materials and methods to fit the needs and technological developments of modern society.

The Steiner House, Vienna, 1910, designed by Adolf Loos. *Electa Archives*

The International Influence of The Avant-Garde Modern Movement

From the late nineteenth century, an efficient organization of cultural exhibitions, associations, books and journals disseminated verbal and visual images formed from heterogeneous experiments of the Western culture of the time. Cultural contacts were exceptionally intense as movements and artists inspired each other in many ways. Through these resources, those well acquainted with one another, or with their ideas, spurred each other on. These resources of the Modern Movement quickly became the style guides for the Moderne.

Exhibitions, Organizations and Competitions

In 1898, the Deutsche Werkstate was founded by Karl Schmidt of Dresden. The firm was inspired initially by English Arts & Crafts models, but moved toward mass production and standardization during the first decade of the twentieth century, and in 1910, it put low-priced unit furniture on the market.

All the Art Nouveau ferment surfaced in the first decade of the twentieth century. It was displayed in the universal exhibition in Paris in 1900 and then the international exhibition in Turin in 1902. In France, the Société des Artistes Décorateurs, the first such organization, was established in 1901. Then, in Germany, the Deutsche Werkbund was founded in 1907, coordinating all the *avant-garde* experiments in the field of applied arts. This exhibition allowed a periodic comparison between the productions of the vari-

One view of The Bauhaus School, Dessau, 1925-26, designed by Walter Gropius. *Museum of Modern Art*

Another view of The Bauhaus School, Dessau, 1925-26, designed by Walter Gropius. *Museum of Modern Art*

ous countries. It addressed the balance of artistic expression versus machine/industrial organization, with the aim of setting standards while accepting industrial production.

The next development came out of America when, in 1922, the *Chicago Tribune* organized the first competition of world importance for a new building. A milestone in the history of the Modern Movement, the competition included designs by Gropius, Loos, and Max Taut. The prize-winners were traditional. First prize went to Raymond Hood for a soaring Gothic style. Second prize went to Eliel Saarinen, who settled in Chicago the following year and built with subtle references to medieval styles.

A few years later, in 1925, at the Exposition Internationale des Arts Décoratifs et Industriels Modernes in Paris, Austrian Josef Hoffmann presented a pavilion design expressing the Viennese Secessionist style and reminiscent of his well-published Palais Stoclet in Brussels. Meanwhile, Swiss-born French architect Le Corbusier (Charles-Edouard Jeanneret) made use of his French pavilion devoted to *L'Esprit Nouveau* to build an element of the *immeuble-villas* and display the overall organization of his modern space for living. In the same exhibition, he presented his first concrete town-planning proposal: the *Plan Voisin*, for contemporary living in the center of Paris.

In 1927, the Deutsche Werkbund exhibition at Stuttgart presented what was considered the first coherent review of the Modern Movement to the public. It clearly showed the common aims of many architects from many different countries. This same attitude continued in Berlin at the 1928 exhibition, and at the international exhibit in Barcelona in 1929, which featured Mies van der Rohe's German pavilion. The new international modern mode was expressed in Paris at a Werkbund exhibition in 1930, and in Berlin in 1931 at a German exhibit. The Parisian press, which covered all of these exhibitions – foreign and local – saw a unity with the German exhibitions and liked the presentation of an alternative to the traditional way of living.

In fact, the new internationalism brought the varied arts together in Paris, and there in 1929, the Union des Artistes Modernes was founded. It included painters, sculptors, and architects such as Robert Mallet-Stevens and Pierre Chareau. In 1931, they were joined by Le Corbusier, Gropius, Willem Marinus Dudok, and, in 1932, by Andre Lurcat and Peter Sartoris.

Publications

Ideas of the European *avant-garde* spread across continents by numerous publications. From the 1880s, Belgian developments spread via the weekly review *L'Art Moderne*, founded in 1881 and lasting up to World War I. The publication also included notices and presentations of van de

Ludwig Mies van der Rohe's design of the German Pavilion at the 1929 Barcelona Exhibition. *Dr. Franz Stoedtner*

Velde's lecture series. In England, *The Studio* began in 1893 (publishing the works of Scotsman Mackintosh) and the *Architectural Review* was established in 1896. In Germany, there was *Jugendstil* magazine, *Decorative Kunst*, and the review *Pan*, as well as notices of German art dealer S. Bing's shop in Paris called *L'Art Nouveau*. There were traditional German publications such as *Moderne Bauformen*, and *Wasmuth Menatshafte fur Baukunst und Stadtebau,* which in 1910 exhibited and published American Frank Lloyd Wright's work in Berlin. In France, there were both academic and *avant garde* reviews, such as *Arts et Decoration*, *L'art décoratif*, and *Revue des arts décoratifs*. In Vienna, after the Secession group began in 1898, there was its publication, *Ver Sacrum*.

Even at the height of the movement, some *avant-garde* journals ended for various unrelated reasons, such as the French *L'Esprit Nouveau* in 1925, the Dutch *De Stijl* in 1928, and the German *Bauhaus Review* in 1929. In their places, new *avant-garde* publications arose in the form of Germany's *Die Form*, 1929, from the Deutsche Werkbund, and in 1930, France's *L'Architecture d'Aujourd'hui.*

Among book publications were Wagner's *Moderne Architecktur,* 1894; Gropius' *Internationale Architecktur*, 1925; essays by John Russell Hitchcock and Bruno Taut, 1929, and by Charles H. Cheney, 1930; the *Wasmuth Lexicon der Baukunst*, 1929-32; and in 1930, the first volume of Le Corbusier's work from 1910 to 1929.

England became the obvious location to disseminate ideas to English-speaking countries, as well as a stopping-off place for the European émigrés. In 1927, Le Corbusier published an English version of *Vers une Architecture* and, in 1929, did the same for his book *Urbanisme*. After leaving the Bauhaus, Gropius settled in London, where he associated with Edwin Maxwell-Fry and was later joined by Marcel Breuer. In the 1920s, Erich Mendelsohn was published in the English press and his book *Amerika*, 1926, was published in English. In 1934, Mendelsohn settled in London for a few years, collaborating with émigré Serge Chermayeff. In addition, émigrés Peter Behrens and Berthold Lubetkin ended up living and working – as well as being published – in England.

English was also the language of the leading history of the Modern Movement, penned by Hungarian critic Nikolaus Pevsner, who lived in Germany but immigrated to England in 1936. His *Pioneers of the Modern Movement from William Morris to Walter Gropius* was the first attempt to trace the history and influences of modern architecture. Pevsner showed the intellectual and moral source formulated by Morris coalescing with the technical experiments of engineers, along with the experiments of artists and contributions of *avant-garde* architects between 1890 and 1914.

From Ballets Russes To Modern Jazz: Moderne Distinctions

> The rapid spread of the new architectural repertoire and its more or less superficial imitations posed a serious difficulty for the theoreticians and protagonists of the modern movements. It had been shown that the use of certain forms did not guarantee the acceptance of certain principles, but could be turned to various ends, contradictory among themselves.[11]
>
> —Leonardo Benevolo

The search for a new formal language started as a protest against the devalued motifs of historicism. In 1908, when Loos wrote "Ornament and Crime," he demanded a formal purge: "Cultural evolution means that we have to eliminate any ornament from our artifacts," he claimed. "It shows the greatness of our age that it is unable to produce a new ornament."[12] Loos was set against traditional beauty, believing that utility or function was the only value of the new age. Yet, during the same period, Piet Mondrian introduced the "pure plastic art" of Purism which satisfied the aims of Functionalism, as it eliminated the traditional motif and presented primary color and voids as new space-defining elements that were beauty in themselves.

Likewise, Loos' conflict of rational utility versus beauty would be at odds with German architect Walter Gropius' Modern Movement point of view, where reason was a regulating principle, in which utility and beauty were reconciled, since the true value of things was a product of man's creation. Functionalists like Gropius aimed at a true correspondence between form and content. To solve this problem, an open system of symbols was required, and that is why Gropius refused to use the word *style*, preferring the term *method*.

It was nearly impossible to create an open system of symbols without references to traditional styles. Forms such as closed corners, frames around doors and windows, arches and sloping roofs were rejected because they reminded one of the past and were considered part of a closed system of symbols. Functionalist architecture, therefore, became an "architecture of exclusion," a style which could not account for all aspects of human existence. Eventually an understanding of the principles of open symbolism allowed even the forms of the past as part of the pluralism that developed after World War II. But during the 1920s and '30s, architects who remained interested in topological organization and plastic articulation, such as Erich Mendelsohn, Hans Haring, and Hans Scharoun, remained outside the mainstream Modern Movement and were frequently labeled Expressionist.

However, because the Modern Movement was an operative choice that only later became a theory, numerous architects and designers retained old conceptual habits. As far as non-technical matters were concerned, they were highly imaginative. They even welcomed the plastic contributions of Expressionists and Futurists, appropriately restrained. In addition, many architects of the younger generation temporarily absorbed the elements of their rationalist teachers and contemporaries, but produced a watered-down version of modern architecture which was extremely successful in Germany and elsewhere, presenting themselves as mediators between old and new. And as modern architecture reached a peak of prestige and popularity, even some architects who had undergone academic educations reduced their Classical references to bare allusions.

Walter Gropius and Adolf Meyer's competition entry for the Chicago Tribune Building, 1922.
Architectural Photographing Co., Chicago

Opposite page:
The Chicago Tribune Building, 1922-24, by Raymond Hood of the firm of Hood and Howell, is a predecessor of the American Art Deco skyscrapers.
Architectural Photographing Co., Chicago

Art Deco From France

Because of the authority they had gained during the first decade of the twentieth century, the Viennese were influential throughout Europe. Appealing to the French designers of the Art Deco style, Josef Hoffmann continued to dictate to European taste as far as furnishings were concerned, even after the collapse of the Wiener Werkstatte in 1933 due to the economic crisis. However, the Art Deco style truly belonged to France. It had its roots in the exotic style of Sergei Diaghilev's pre-1914 Ballets Russes, with its brilliant costumes and stage sets that were seen in Paris in the first decade of the century. The colorful idiom was boosted by the 1925 Paris Exposition Internationale des Arts Décoratifs et Industriels Modernes, from which it took its name.

Ballets Russes' production of Scheherazade at the Opera in Paris, 1910 with costumes by Leon Bakst. Director Sergei Diaghilev introduced Russian art and culture to the west, via Paris, the cultural center of Europe. *Bibliotheque nationale, Paris*

Although it was not strictly an architectural style, Art Deco became a way of reconciling Moderne buildings of the Expressionist variety and the stripped Classicism of Auguste Perret and his disciples with the decorative and craft traditions that still derived strength from the Art Nouveau. The heavy colorful, ceramic forms of Art Deco were especially popular in France for shops and cinemas.

This new angular style was showcased at the famous 1925 Paris Exposition intended to display works of new inspiration and real originality. Reproductions, imitations, and counterfeits of ancient styles were to be strictly prohibited. It included works by Hoffmann, Mallet-Stevens, Lurcat and Michel Roux-Spitz, as well as Le Corbusier's *L'Esprit Nouveau* pavilion and city plan. Le Corbusier's work expressed true Modern style, but his allusion to ships with pipe rail and circular windows and planar white stucco walls would fuel the ornamental Art Deco label. Truly, the 1925 exhibit was not meant to be simply decorative – but this is what populist culture had taken from it. Following the Paris exposition, this new style arrived in America, where it lent itself to architecture, design, and industrial design. "Style Moderne," as it was first called, proved particularly popular with businesses that wanted their buildings to have a fresh, contemporary image.

As Perret refreshed the Classical idiom in France by means of concrete structural technique that had swept the country, his work influenced the production of numerous prominent urban buildings of the 1930s that straddled the border between stripped Classicism and Modern style and could be found in cities such as Paris and Geneva.

Another French Art Deco architect was Henri Sauvage, who gave up designing in an Art Nouveau style and became preoccupied with the form of the urban apartment block. His colorfully clad flats in the Rue Vavin, Paris, 1912-13, developed a stepped section which provided balconies, light, and air throughout a building. The many stepped sections derive from dramatic sketches by the Italian Futurist Antonio Sant'Elia. Sauvage also designed Cinema Gambetta, Paris, 1920, and with his friend, Art Nouveau architect Frantz Jourdain, transformed the La Samaritaine Store, Paris, with heavier elevations in the late 1920s.

As mentioned earlier, Tony Garnier's importance belongs to the history of town planning. His *Cité Industrielle* was an ideal project begun in 1901 and published in 1917. It depicted an industrial city for 35,000 people, united by a flat-roofed cubic formalism and planned with rigid zoning distinctions between home and workplace, center and suburb, pedestrian and motor traffic. In his native Lyon, Garnier was able to fulfill his Utopian city plan when he was employed to lay out the market area in 1908. It included Les Mouches, 1909, of which the stepped and steel-framed Art Deco hall had a 262-foot span.

A fine example of the mixture of Classical and decorative styles is the City Library, Toulouse, built for a socialist municipal administration by city architect Jean Montariol. It includes spangles of glass in the reading room ceiling and sculptural reliefs of workers along the front façade. Public buildings of circa 1925-35 in France and Italy often assumed such didactic decorations with ponderous symbolic messages. Official Classicism in these years gradually became simpler and more stripped under the influence of Perret – for example, the architecture of Albert Laprade in his 1929 Museum of the Colonies (now Museum of African and Oceanic Art), Paris, and his Parisian Citroen Store of the same year.

Garage in rue Ponthieu, Paris, 1905, designed by Auguste Perret. *Dr. Franz Stoedtner*

French houses and apartment buildings of the period, though often touched by Art Deco, mostly adhered to a quiet Classicism, with the addition of pilasters and cherubs on relief panels to assert their claims to culture. Roger Expert built four such villas in the seaside town of Arcachon, 1924-27, as well as the French Embassy, Belgrade, 1930. However, the most famous house in Paris of the Art Deco period is the Maison de Verre (or the Dalsace House), 1928-32. It is a Moderne example of the "machine for living" (Le Corbusier's terms), with outstanding use of glass and metal. Its designers were Pierre Chareau and the Dutchman Bernard Bijvoet.

Other important *avant-garde* designers in France of the Art Deco style include Mallet-Stevens, Roux-Spitz, and Eileen Gray. With Jean Bacovici, Gray designed two magnificent houses at Roquebrunne, near Nice, taking full advantage of the Modern Movement's concern for sun and light. Mallet-Stevens designed a cul-de-sac of houses (now the Rue Mallet-Stevens) in Paris, 1926-27, that were influenced by Loos and the Dutch De Stijl designers, as well as the large Villa Trappenard, at Sceaux, 1930. He was active as a designer of film sets and shops as well. Roux-Spitz also enjoyed a position between Art Deco and *avant-garde* modernism. Among his apartment buildings in Paris, 35 Boulevard des Italiens over a Ford showroom, 1931, is notable. He also built himself a fine villa at Dinard with murals by Louis Bousquet.

France did not have an authoritarian regime like that of the Nazis, Fascists, or Stalinists, which would have inevitably come into conflict with modern architecture. However, after 1934, there was a radicalization of political struggle and increasing economic unease that was reflected in a drop in building production. Modern architects were cut off almost entirely from any opportunity of work. While Le Corbusiér and Lurcat were essentially unemployed, a group of new Modern architects found success by producing watered-down versions of the Modern style or a compromise of Perret-like Classicism. Even former functionalists became inclined toward classicizing the monumental, as visible in the later pavilions of Mallet-Stevens. Whether pure examples or diluted versions, the body of French Art Deco work was inspirational to an international audience via publications and first-hand Parisian tours throughout the mid-1920s, '30s, and '40s.

Streamline Moderne From Germany

In Germany, a Streamline version of the Modern Movement was produced by Erich Mendelsohn, a Prussian-born architect whose sources varied from the dynamics of aristocratic costume design of the Russian ballet to the sketches of Italian Futurist Antonio Sant Elia to the Streamline Classicism of Otto Wagner and Joseph Maria Olbrich of the Viennese Secession. His first sketches of 1914 were inspired by the style of Wagner and Olbrich, and those made during World War I and shortly thereafter were almost symbolist in character and seemed suited to the contemporary Expressionist movement.

Maison de Verre ("Glass House," also known as Dalsace House), Paris, 1928-32, designed by Pierre Chareau. *P. Chareau*

In the late 1910s and '20s, Mendelsohn had an enormous influence in Germany, greater than that of any other architect of his generation. In 1919, he exhibited his visionary architectural sketches at the Cassirer Gallery and they were later assembled into book form by the editor of *Wasmuth*. And in 1920, he transformed one of these aggressive moving sketches into reality when he was given the opportunity to design Einstein's astronomical observatory tower at Potsdam. The impression is of a fluid mass with the tower and its curving, dynamic base. The most suitable material for such a plastic shape was reinforced concrete; however, there were no moulds available for curved and flowing forms, so the tower was made with brick with a covering of cement. The work thus became the mere illustration of an abstract modern concept.

Einstein Tower, Neubabelsberg (near Potsdam), 1921, by Erich Mendelsohn. *Landesbildstelle, Berlin*

Mendelsohn's later works include the Berliner Tageblatt building of 1923, in which the plasticity of the building was marked with decorative strips that accented every protruding point and curved element. Between 1926 and 1928, he continued with this format for a series of three Schocken department stores, where he also used the continuous windows as the decorative strip. Mendelsohn was committed to the fact that these dramatic external effects came from the internal organism and his later work, the Universuum Theatre in Berlin, 1934, did much to make this point of expressing the nature of the building in its volume and form.

Mendelsohn had not come from the Bauhaus, nor was he directly influenced by it, but he found there a common point of reference. While his first work, like his sketches, had its origins in a different cultural environment, his later works nonetheless expressed the same basic unity of purpose with the German Modern Movement in terms of clarity, flexibility, and spatial volume.

Between Mendelsohn's first visit to America in 1924 and his move there in 1941, architects, critics, and historians became aware of, and influenced by, his style. Mendelsohn's work was first published in the U.S. in the October 1921 issue of *Dial Magazine* and he met Norman Bel Geddes when he came to New York in 1924, giving him a copy of his 1923 *Structures and Sketches*. Mendelsohn gave his impressions of America in an August 22, 1926, issue of *The New York Times Magazine*. In the same year, Mendelsohn and his works began to interest an American audience. Frank Lloyd Wright was quoted in Francis Onderdonk, Jr.'s 1926 *The Ferro-Concrete Style*, describing Mendelsohn's Einstein Tower as "a purely plastic structure," and Paul Frankl included him in his popular 1928 *New Dimensions, The Decorative Arts of Today in Words and Pictures*.

In 1929, Mendelsohn's work was exhibited in the "Contempora Exposition of Art and Industry" at New York Art Center. Bel Geddes wrote the catalog entry for Mendelsohn's sketches, models, and photographs of built work. He described the German as the "ideal" architect, having "...the dramatist's instinct...[he] adds the emotional quality that attracts and inspires humanity for future time."[13] Frank Lloyd Wright and architectural renderer Hugh Ferris also acknowledged Mendelsohn's work when they gave a radio interview about the exhibit and reviewed it in the November 1930 *Architectural Forum*. Wright wrote:

> ...[I]t seems to me that individuality is one of the greatest and most valuable things to be found in [the exhibition]. Mr. Mendelsohn's exhibition itself marks it. That exhibition is romantic, a powerful realization of the picturesqueness of our special machine brutalities, and one may see a fresh simplicity in his sentiment and a vigorous power of expression in nearly everything he does.[14]

New York industrial designer Paul Wiener was a confirmed Mendelsohn follower, and along with Wright and Ferris, he wrote about his mentor in the November 1930 issue of *Architectural Forum*, declaring his work as pointing to the future of architectural development.

While Henry-Russell Hitchcock included Mendelsohn in his 1929 *Modern Architecture: Romanticism and Re-Integration*, he somewhat dismissed the German as an Expressionist reveling in the influence of machines. On the other hand, another New York industrial designer, Sheldon Cheney, thoroughly praised Mendelsohn in his very popular *The New World Architecture* of 1930, writing that Mendelsohn "made buildings expressive of the 'feel' of the machine" and acknowledging his stylistic influence on commercial architecture.[15]

Aldous Huxley also appreciated Mendelsohn's work and wrote about him in the March 1930 issue of *Creative Art*. There, too, the brilliance of Mendelsohn's commercial work was recognized: "His big shops with their bold alternation of planes and sweeping curves, their square or streamlined towers, their insistent striation..."[16]

With such publications and introductions through Wright, Ferris, Bel Geddes, Cheney, Hitchcock, and Huxley, Mendelsohn's reputation and his images traveled across America, sometimes anonymously, as in the April 1934 issue of *Scientific American*. The Depression also hastened the anonymous copying of Mendelsohnian elements, such as his simply curved architectural and decorative forms, glass-enclosed stair-towers, slab-like signage, circular windows, horizontal mouldings, shiny metal and glass materials.

When young architects who watered down Modernism adopted various Mendelsohnian elements, they accepted new formal contributions without involving themselves in any of the basic problems or addressing the initial concepts. With new building types, such as department stores and cinemas, they easily adopted formal elements as symbols as well as structure. They used them as a style guide as easily as adopting a diluted Modern style from the works of Gropius or Mies van der Rohe.

Erich Mendelsohn's Project Drawing for Schocken Department Store, 1927. *Landesbildstelle, Berlin*

Erich Mendelsohn's Schocken Department Store (later Merkur Store), Stuttgart, 1927. *Landesbildstelle, Berlin*

Along the same derivative lines, in 1932, a significant confirmation of the position of the Viennese with regard to the Modern Movement was offered in Vienna by the Werkbund Exhibition. A model district of two- and three-story houses was built and designed by Hoffmann, Loos, and twenty-two other Austrians, along with Lurcat from France, Gerrit Rietveld from Holland, Richard Neutra from America, and Hans Haring from Germany. While these had the flat roofs and white walls of previous model exhibitions, they had a different spirit, which was considered formalist and escapist. In addition to the decorative bias, the housing projects seemed to abandon the ideal of integrating workers' quarters into the city and presented examples for semi-rural suburbia.

In the vernacularization of a style, basic symbolic forms usually possess a Gestalt quality and the modes of organization are related to so-called Gestalt laws, such as similarity, proximity, continuity, and closure. Vernacular architecture is not simply a direct reflection of physical conditions and needs, but possesses the distinguishing properties of symbol systems. Both vernacular architecture and monumental building have common roots and serve the same symbolic function and both express the values and needs in a public form of life. The difference is that monumental architecture represents a higher level of abstraction and conception.

In examining the Viennese exhibition and the influence of the commercial works of Mendelsohn, it is revealing to note the distortions the modern repertoire underwent in this process of vernacularization and transcription. One constant was the use of smooth white walls. While imitators accepted this, they were concerned not to let the wall surface lose its physicality, treating it in such a way to retain texture. Plaster was left rough to be affected by the light. In fact, there was a widespread use of coverings of stone slabs, so that differences of plane and color would create a subtle chiaroscuro. Window surrounds often were made to project rhythmical patterns and shadows on the wall. The same dramatic attitude was also recognizable in graphics, in the charcoal drawings of elevations, as well as in the style of architectural photographs taken almost frontally, in direct light with marked foreshortening, as in the photographs of Lucia Moholy-Nagy.

Some of the housing built for the 1932 Vienna Werkbundsielung was considered "formalist." This set of apartments was designed by J.F. Dex, W. Sobotka, O. Strand, and Josef Hoffmann. *A. Sartoris*

From Art Deco Tower To Streamline Slab:

Moderne In America

The publications and exhibitions of the *avant-garde* Europeans were noticed in America. However, the dynamic of the American scene at the turn of the century to early twentieth century was led by an open-minded industrialism with a nod to the persistence of conventions as then proscribed by Horatio Greenough, a contemporary of John Ruskin. Ruskin, too, was influential in the United States, but partially, through his medievalism and his anti-Classicism as it affected external results rather than the social imperative recognized by William Morris in Europe.

It had seemed that the American *avant-garde* did not survive intact: The Chicago School lost its distinctive style after the 1893 Exposition and the California School was dispersed in the same way after the San Diego Exposition of 1915. Only the ready-made rules of historical styles seemed to survive. Yet, "eclectic perfection" seemed to be an American strength with singular coherence when it was as notable as Henry Hobson Richardson's neo-Romanesque, which was superior to the European models.

But eclecticism faded in the face of modern life. The change took place in the years around 1930 and coincided with economic circumstances. At this point, the Modern Movement made its contribution felt as the American economic crisis coincided with the European political crisis and numbers of talented artists and architects moved from Europe to the United States. However, the contribution was not smooth or continuous. The movement was often received just as another European style and the Americans imitated the new models just as superficially as they had historic styles. While the goal of the European movement was to have an architecture that overcame national differences, in America these European architects confronted a nation where real international experiment and discussion could take place.

From 1919 to 1929, American building production was intense and cities changed to concentrations of central business centers while simultaneously extending into the suburbs with one-family houses – some even prefabricated in Colonial style. Most frequently, the cities' skyscrapers were full of technical advances, but they were wrapped in eclectic garb, particularly the soaring Gothic, a favorite of Raymond M. Hood, William Van Alen, and the firms Shreve, Lamb and Harmon in New York and Holabird and Root in Chicago. These have since been labeled the Art Deco skyscrapers.

While the earliest European influences felt in America came in the guise of a competition in 1922, it asserted the eclectic historicism. Nonetheless, the *Chicago Tribune* competition offered the visions of many Modern Movement architects such as Gropius, Loos, and Max Taut. Hood's winning Gothic design was completed in 1924. It was the favorite of most architects and critics, and Chicago architect Louis Sullivan even wrote a tribute to it. The stepped form was plastically modeled with vertical elements and gently receding volumes. The style became instantly popular in New York. There, renderer Hugh Ferriss used it to model his dramatic studies of the massing volumes dictated by the still-new 1916 step-back zoning laws.

Another vaguely medieval tower was the *Tribune* competition's second prize winner by émigré Eliel Saarinen. His design and later work, as well as that of the German Expressionists and contemporary French decorative designers, were also significant influences on this body of Art Deco skyscrapers. Sources such as these were synthesized to include not only aspects of eclecticism and Modern style, but also Classical qualities.

These Art Deco skyscrapers represented strength as dynamic, three-dimensional objects, offering vivid symbols of prosperity and promise. Their vertical piers led to varied arrangements of setbacks calculated to protect the air rights of neighboring buildings. Hood, in his Daily News Building, New York, 1929-30, gave sculptural form and character to repetitive façades by the application of the requirement of setbacks. Lavish ornament remained subordinate to bold masses which reflected the steel frame behind them. The results were considered to be the epitome of modern innovation, but they were also depicted as latter-day versions of ancient cultures and embodied a spirit of opulence and solidity inherited from their academic traditions. New York and Chicago were the primary cities where the ideal Art Deco towers were developed. Among the best known examples were, in New York, the Chrysler Building, 1928-30, by William Van Alen, and the Empire State Building, 1929-31, by Shreve, Lamb and Harmon, and, in Chicago, the Board of Trade Building, 1929-30, by Holabird and Root. The type was superbly employed in numerous other cities from the mid-1920s until the Depression, as was seen in the now-demolished Richfield Building in Los Angeles, 1928-30, by Morgan, Walls & Clements.

During these few years, Art Deco skyscrapers had a major impact on the character of large and small cities alike. They were appealing for their stylized decorative panels and spandrels, their handsome metalwork, and their classically-inspired but modern sculptures and reliefs. Many were coloristic with stained terra-cotta ornament, silver or gold metals, hued paint, stone, and concrete. And there was the typical juxtaposition of light and dark details and smooth and textured elements. Clients and corporations became caught up in this Modernistic style – the flashier, the more popular. It was a crowd-pleasing style, indiscriminate of how many sources it borrowed from – whether French, Assyrian, Mayan, or Modern. A whole repertory of angular and curvilinear forms developed, none of it specifically related to historic styles. There were chevrons, zigzags and floral fields, faceted crystalline forms, stripes of glass, tile, mosaic and brass. In metal, terra-cotta, concrete, or stone, the ornament was woven into the exterior walls and piled up into rooftop crestings. It covered entrance porticoes, lobbies and elevator areas. These Art Deco flourishes were found in the commercial buildings of most large cities and in many countries, leading one 1920s journal to call the style "universalism."[17]

The Chrysler Building, New York, 1930, designed by William Van Alen, is considered a key example of America's Art Deco skyscrapers. *Courtesy Jack Kent Cooke*

However, skyscraper development took a different turn in the work of Bertram Goodhue, whose State Capital in Lincoln, Nebraska, 1921-31, expanded on the idea of a block surmounted by a tower, which was a widely used form in American public buildings since the 1870s. Approaching the form with a Modern sensibility, Goodhue exaggerated both parts and intensified the relationship by the abstraction of the form and its bold scale. The contrast of the ground-hugging base and the soaring tower creates a strong civic character. While there is a sense of newness about the design, it still retains allusions to ancient Rome, the Near East, Byzantium and medieval Europe, as well as having a Beaux-Arts cross-in-square ground plan. These same elements were visible in Goodhue's 1922-26 Central Library in Los Angeles.

Los Angeles Public Library (now the Richard J. Riordan Central Library), 1922-26, Bertram Goodhue and Carleton M. Winslow. Goodhue's design offered an alternative to the typical Art Deco skyscraper; it presented a stripped Classical form that related to the future Streamline style. *Tom Zimmerman Collection*

About 1930, the Modern repertoire began to spread even further. The Modern Movement was controversially introduced into America by the Swiss émigré William Lescaze, who worked with the American George Howe. The two of them built private houses applying the rationalist approach inflexibly and, in 1931, they were given the commission for an important commercial structure, the Philadelphia Savings Fund Society Building, completed in 1932. The Modern method radically changed the traditional organization of the skyscraper: instead of a tower, their work was a sleek steel-and-glass slab denoting its structure. A number of other architects seized on the conception. Hood, in particular, adopted it for his last New York skyscrapers: the Daily News building of 1930, the McGraw-Hill building of 1931, and the Rockefeller Center, begun in 1932. All of these had the smooth walls, horizontal copings, and cubist volumes. Although it was developed in the 1930s and appeared occasionally throughout the decade, it was not until the mid-1950s that the vertical slab wrapped in glass replaced the Art Deco tower as a symbol of business prestige.

While the Modern style of Howe and Lescaze made a strong impact on commercial architecture, Modern Movement architecture was largely introduced to most Americans by Henry-Russell Hitchcock and Philip Johnson in their exhibit and book, *The International Style*, 1932. Although it fueled many discussions, it did not show the full gamut of European Modernism. Considered highly selective, it eliminated Futurism, Russian Constructivism, the Amsterdam School, and German Expressionism from the overall Modern Movement while it extracted the social purpose and rational passion behind the European development. So once again, with the blessings of New York's Museum of Modern Art and most American Modern scholars of the period, it was easy for American architects to denature the European sources, separating them from their meanings and using them picturesquely for any purpose.

The Philadelphia Savings Fund Society Building, Philadelphia, 1931-32, designed by George Howe and William Lescaze, was one of the first Streamline slab skyscrapers. *William Lescaze Associates*

The otherwise undecorated, largely concrete structures produced under this influence in the manner of Bauhaus, Modern Movement, or International School are often mistakenly called Art Deco. But the lack of any ornament, polychromy, or ornamental metalwork generally disqualifies them from being classified under that rubric, at least to purists. However, these works fall comfortably under the definition of the Streamline phase of the Moderne. And by the early 1930s, the taste for streamlined shapes became more noticeable, inspired by modern transport design. Nautical details from the new luxury liners, such as curved walls, circular windows or windows with rounded corners, and handrails of tubular metal, became more popular and worked well in these denatured offspring of the International Style/ Modern Movement examples.

Industrial Designers

The Moderne, in either its Art Deco or Streamline phases, does not completely make up a school or period of architecture in the way the Modern Movement or International Style has. On the whole, the best of these works have been designed by American architects trained in the traditional manner and their structures take the practical route in terms of structural techniques, materials, and services. What made the Moderne Style unique was its interest in the total package of design: architecture and its interior, and the industrially-produced object and furnishing. While the Bauhaus was educating and promoting this new profession in Europe, in the mid-1920s, industrial designers firmly established this new profession in New York. Walter Dorwin Teague began his activities in 1926, followed by Norman Bel Geddes and Raymond Loewy in 1927. The American Union of Decorative Artists and Craftsmen (AUDAC) started there in 1927 in response to the circumstance of 1925, when Secretary Herbert Hoover had to decline the United States' participation in the Paris Exposition because it had no modern designs to submit. The organization was begun by such designers as Donald Deskey, Paul T. Frankl, Gilbert Rohde, Kem Weber, Edward Steichen, and Rockwell Kent. Many of the new designers were enamored of Futurism and its interest in speed and modernity and in it they recognized the first European *avant-garde* culture that held the possibility of a new synthesis of the arts.

The Art Deco 1920s and the Streamline 1930s opened up novel architectural uses for new man-made materials such as chrome, glass, vitrolite, polished bronze, and stainless steel. With this integrated vision, an architectural structure could be perceived as a sculptural gem. Lessons could be learned from these industrial design artists who were graphic designers, package designers, advertising illustrators, poster-artists, window-display artists, and theatrical designers. Men such as Teague, Loewy, and Bel Geddes, as well as Deskey, Russel Wright, Henry Dreyfuss, Frankl, and Albert Frey elevated standards of taste and professionalism. Not only were cars, trains, and ocean liners streamlined for aerodynamic purposes, but the style was applied to furniture, appliances, typography, graphics, jewelry, and fashion as well. Streamlining represented modernity, economy, and efficiency, in addition to aerodynamics. It directed greater awareness of space and sculptural form. Streamlining came to symbolize progress and the shape of a better future, especially when an economic depression dampened the public spirit at the end of the 1920s.

Opposite page:
The Maddux Airlines Building, 1928, with interiors designed by émigré industrial designer Jock Peters. The murals depict the various transport vehicles that were popular in Art Deco decorations and inspired the Streamline structures of the next few decades. *California State Library*

6
BAKERSFIELD FRESNO SAN FRANCISCO
5
SAN BERNARDINO PALM SPRINGS IMPERIAL VALLEY CALEXICO
4
SAN DIEGO AGUA CALIENTE
3
RACE SPECIAL SAN DIEGO AGUA CALIENTE
1
FROM SAN FRANCISCO

"The Streamliner Passing Through a California Orange Grove," postcard from 1934. *Tom Zimmerman Collection*

The 1934 Streamliner Train in Los Angeles. *Pius Zimmerman; Tom Zimmerman Collection*

Depression Moderne

The worst of the economic crisis hit America in 1929, giving way to decisive changes in politics and cultural customs. The Great Depression dealt a final death blow to the old skyscrapers and the American Beaux-Arts movement. When Franklin Delano Roosevelt was elected president for the first time in 1932, he quickly implemented his program of political and economic reforms. More than anything, his PWA (Public Works Administration), WPA (Works Progress Administration), and CCC (Civilian Conservation Corps) projects spread the Moderne style across America, using sleek, streamlined forms in chrome and formica for institutional projects, gatehouses, and public toilets. With bridges, roads, and dams throughout the country, there seemed a new kind of architecture – directly functional while implying the symbolic presence of monumentality. Moderne institu-

Interior of the Science Building by Paul Cret, The Century of Progress Fair, 1933, Chicago. *Architectural Photographing Co., Chicago*

The Social Science Building designed by Raymond Hood, The Century of Progress Fair, 1933, Chicago. *Architectural Photographing Co., Chicago*

tional architecture went back to the representational powers of the Classical styles, sometimes in full dress as the new Supreme Court Building or the National Gallery in Washington, and other times as "starved Classicism" or Depression Moderne with ornament simplified into angular accents that recede into the structure, and columns and sculpture held to a minimum.

Introducing the Streamline Style to the nation at the height of the Depression was the 1932-33 Century of Progress World Fair in Chicago, which showed Americans how to build with plywood, chicken-wire, and bright color. The Fair's Committee was made up of Harvey Wiley Corbett, Arthur Brown, Jr., Paul P. Cret, Raymond Hood, Ralph Walker, Edward H. Bennett, Hubert Burnham, and John Holabird. Louis Skidmore was Chief of Design and Joseph Urban was in charge of Architectural Color. By 1939, the sophistication of form and material finish of the structures of the New York World's Fair revealed the maturation of the style. The lead was taken, not by the architects who master-planned the project, but by the industrial designers – Norman Bel Geddes, Henry Dreyfuss, Walter Dorwin Teague, and Raymond Loewy – who designed the '39 Fair as a Streamline Moderne world, best displayed in the ideal cities of Dreyfuss' "Democracity" and Bel Geddes' "Futurama."

Under the New Deal reforms, the radically changed conditions for American architecture and planning altered the scene and allowed the concepts of beauty, utility, and method of the Modern Movement to deeply penetrate into the realities of American life. It was a far greater lesson than any learned through the controversies of the *avant-garde* or the formal propaganda of the Museum of Modern Art.

The Sears Building by Nimmons, Carr & Wright, The Century of Progress Fair, 1933, Chicago. *Architectural Photographing Co., Chicago*

Norman Bel Geddes's design of the General Motors Highway exhibition hall and street intersection from the City of Tomorrow exhibit, New York World's Fair, 1939. Bel Geddes was one of a group of industrial designers who were chiefly responsible for the design of the fair. *Richard Garrison*

NBC
KNBH
TELEVISION
CHANNEL 4
AD 1938
NBC RADIO CITY NBC
VINE ST.
BOULEVARD LOAN CO.

An early example of the Classical Moderne that influenced Los Angeles' 1930s PWA "stripped" Classical buildings: the Pacific Coast Stock Exchange, 1929-30, designed by Samuel E. Lunden; John & Donald B. Parkinson, consulting architects. *Tom Zimmerman Collection*

Opposite page:
NBC Television and Radio Building, Los Angeles, 1938-39, John C. Austin (now demolished). *Tom Zimmerman Collection*

I. L.A.'s Deco and Streamline Styles In Context

A Socio-Political Note

In Los Angeles, the era that created the stylistic fashions of the Art Deco 1920s and the Streamline 1930s also produced a parallel rise of a true modern architecture in the works of Irving Gill, Frank Lloyd Wright, Richard Neutra, Rudolph Schindler, and a handful of architects who followed their method in the next generation. The era represented an ideological split in architectural terms – one ideology being an elite modern and experimental direction, and the other being a highly popular and accessible psuedo-machine one. There was a parallel in socio-political terms and Mike Davis made this point in his *City of Quartz* when he concluded: "The ultimate world-historical significance – and oddity – of Los Angeles is that it has come to play the double role of utopia *and* dystopia for advanced capitalism."[18]

In exploring Los Angeles as a center of this ideological struggle, Davis traced a critical history of the region whereby the city is recognized as the world capital of a "culture industry," which, since the 1920s, had imported, and accepted as émigrés, myriads of the most talented writers, filmmakers, artists, and visionaries. The city and its alter-ego, Hollywood, became the city of seduction and defeat, the antithesis of critical intelligence.

In the 1920s, when émigrés Theodor Adorno and Max Horkheimer accumulated their data from World War I and wrote their article, "The Culture Industry," they thought (perhaps somewhat indifferently to the peculiar historical forces that had shaped it) that in Los Angeles, they were encountering America in its purest moment. As Davis describes it, "They allowed their image of first sight to become its own myth: Los Angeles as the crystal ball of capitalism's future."[19]

Adorno and Horkeimer described the Culture Industry as a political economy, and they pointed to the tiny boxes of single-family houses as representative of a world-historic mission of the proletariat transformed by "family-centered consumerism" driven by radio jingles and magazine ads that were so important to the spread of the Moderne. They wrote:

> Even now, the older houses just outside the concrete city center look like slums, and the new bungalows on the outskirts are at one with the flimsy structures of world fairs in their praise of technical progress and their built-in demand to be discarded after a short while like empty food cans. Yet the city housing projects designed to perpetuate the individual as a supposedly independent unit in a small hygienic dwelling make him all the more subservient to his adversary – the absolute power of capitalism.[20]

Exile in Southern California had transformed the émigrés' once-hopeful understanding of Modern style in light of capitalism and most, like Adorno and Horkheimer, were suspect of their new situation in this land of sunshine. They clung to their European prejudices and complained about the absence of history, critical intellectuals, and the deeper sense of European-style public places. Los Angeles was an anti-city, a city of suburbs that melded with the Hollywood of false movie sets.

Oppressed minority groups put on the stereotypical dress that secured them a place in the capitalist dream of Los Angeles' Culture Industry: Mexican singers and dancers celebrate the opening of the PWA Moderne Sepulveda Tunnel, 1941, part of the 1939-41 Sepulveda Control Dam, Water Channels and Control Tower designed by United States District Engineer, War Department. *Tom Zimmerman Collection*

In the 1930s, immigrant writer Louis Adamic's famous essay, "Los Angeles! There She Blows!" (*The Outlook*, August 13, 1930), was quoted in "The Enormous Village" chapter of *Laughing in the Jungle* and was widely noticed by the critical public. It exerted a seminal influence on Carey McWilliams, as well as upon Nathanael West, who, in *The Day of the Locust* (1939), developed Adamic's image of Los Angeles' "spiritually and mentally starving" people – the "Folks" versus the ruling class brutality of such leaders as General Otis who drove labor to desperation.

Adamic had chronicled Los Angeles during the oil-crazy 1920s. His insistence on *class violence* in the social and cultural landscapes of Los Angeles was carried in further detail by his close friend, McWilliams, whose *Southern California Country (An Island on the Land)*, 1936, unmasked Booster mythology and recovered the historical roles of labor and oppressed minority groups.

Adamic was aware of both the Moderne derivations and the Modern experiments in architecture. While instinctively uncomfortable in middle-class society, he was part of a genteel, like-minded group of Los Angeles cultural elite who met at book dealer Jack Zeitlin's shops or his home in Echo Park, including architect Lloyd Wright, photographer Edward Weston, critic-librarian Lawrence Clark Powell, and artist Rockwell Kent, among others.

McWilliams' 1936 work completed the debunking of the myth begun by Adamic in his "Los Angeles! There She Blows!" piece. Beginning with a recovery of the Mexican roots of Southern California and the little-known story of genocide and native resistance during the state's formative years of the 1850s and 1860s, McWilliams deconstructed the Mission Myth and its makers. He picked up where Adamic had left off in his exploration of Los Angeles' labor as he integrated historical narrative with his economic and cultural analysis.

Below:
Signs, streets, and beckoning towers became a part of the auto-driven, family-centered consumerism of Los Angeles. Towered commercial one- and two-story buildings located near the crossing of Westwood and Wilshire boulevards, circa 1941. *Tom Zimmerman Collection*

Opposite page:
During the 1920s, '30s, and '40s, Los Angeles became known as a city without a history but filled with bright sunshine, film stars, and ad hoc movie sets: Hollywood starlets Evelyn Ankers and Peggy Moran before the entrance of the Hollywood Bowl in 1941. Sculpture by George Stanley, 1935. *Tom Zimmerman Collection*

OSPC-657

When completed, McWilliams produced a quartet of books that embodied the best exploration of an American regional tradition. It established a commanding regional interpretation in which Los Angeles understood its past through a vital fiction and film history called *noir*. Although some principal *noir* writers, like Raymond Chandler, did little more than generalize the petit-bourgeois resentment against the collapse of the Southern California dream, most claimed Popular Front sympathies. *Noir* has remained the popular anti-myth of Los Angeles.

The tradition of critical writing about Los Angeles since the 1920s indicates strong analytical energies at work. If Los Angeles had become the site of massive subordination of industrialized skill and creative talent to the programs of capital, it had also produced mythologizers, debunkers, and some acute critiques by writers from Nathanael West to Robert Towne to better understand it. To be sure, the forces behind Moderne's Deco and Streamline styles represented a superficial capitalist flourishing that was the convergence of American realism, Weimar expressionism, and existentialized Marxism that was analyzed and exposed in the complex body of literary and cinematic *noir* productions that focused on unmasking "a bright, guilty place," as H.G. Welles called Los Angeles.

Through such creative chroniclers of culture and critical histories, Los Angeles' Moderne architecture in both its Deco and Streamline phases was considered petit-bourgeois and its development in Southern California represented the *noir* myth of the self-made, self-oriented individual surrounding himself with symbols of individualistic hedonism – a world of single family dwellings, freeways, and cars.

This was the analytical context behind the current that architectural historian David Gebhard refers to in his article "About Style, Not Ideology":

> Today if we try to reconstruct what took place in American architecture during the decades of the '20s and '30s, we would more likely than not limit our comments to the work of Frank Lloyd Wright, Richard J. Neutra, and R.M. Schindler, and later to William Lescaze, Gregory Ain, and a few others; we would reveal how well we have been programmed to recite the canonical tale of High Art Modernism....But...a hot battle occurred between Internationalists and the popularizers of the Moderne...

Fortunately, the popularizers of the Moderne in the '20s and '30s avoided much of this spiteful and vicious battle. The exponents of what we today label as Art Deco in the '20s and as Streamline Moderne in the '30s assumed a lackadaisical middle course between High Art Moderns and the Traditionalists. Their course partook of both because their interest lay essentially in design, not ideology. While they certainly hoped their designs would convey a modern view of the past, present, and future, they were involved with the question of visual languages.[21]

Natalie Shivers' recent assessment of the Modern Movement architects in *L.A.'s Early Modernism: Art Architecture Photography*, expands on the body of Gebhard's studies, emphasizing the practical reality of the dearth of modern work in comparison with the great numbers of Moderne structures.

The Fine Line Between Modern and Moderne

With the post-World War I immigration of dozens of Austrian and German architects, designers, dramatists and writers, musicians and filmmakers, Los Angeles became known as "the new Weimar." Moderne Art Deco and Streamline architects were themselves émigrés or knew the work of all of the key American architects and influential émigrés.

Among the architectural leaders of the region, there was, first, Irving Gill, son of a Syracuse contractor who moved to San Diego in 1893. Later, he briefly lived in Los Angeles, where he did a number of projects. While he was inspired by the region's early mission structures, he produced modern forms from them, recognizing the simplicity of the mission's geometric shapes and appreciating the loggias and pergolas that extended the structures into the natural setting. He felt architecture should express the materials and constructional techniques of the modern era and tried tilt-up concrete wall systems, even forming the Concrete Building and Investment Company in 1912, which was based on a 1907 system developed by Robert Aiken. Unappreciated by the cultural capitalists for his blend of local tradition and modernism, Gill's plans for the 1915 San Diego Pan Pacific exposition were passed over for Spanish period style. Nonetheless, Gill's work and ideas lay one of the earliest foundations for the region's Modern Movement.

Frank Lloyd Wright's impact on Los Angeles development is legendary. His modern forms and free use of space attracted a progressive client, Aline Barnsdall, to choose him to design a house and cultural center on Olive Hill. In addition to the innovations of the textile block system of concrete block walls used at the house and the project's unique allusions to Mayan architecture, Wright's project and the cast of characters he brought to it endeared his ideas – as well as European Modern concepts – to the region's cultural elite. In 1920, Wright sent to Los Angeles a young Austrian, Rudolph Schindler, to supervise the construction of the project. He also sent his son Lloyd Wright, who worked on the theater portion with manager/director Richard Ordynski, from Max Reinhardt's theater in Berlin. Set designer – and later one of America's foremost industrial designers – Norman Bel Geddes also participated. The theaters were never built, but Barnsdall's troupe performed before local audiences including Hollywood's directors and producers D.W. Griffith, Cecil B. DeMille, and Erich Von Stroheim.

A progressive kindergarten was also a part of Barnsdall's Olive Hill project, which ended up contributing to the spread of European cultural ideas since the school's liberal free association methods were taught by Rudolph Schindler's wife, Pauline, along with Leah Press Lovell and her sister Harriet Press Freeman. Over the next few years, these fellow teachers' friendships would bear even more fruit. Harriet Freeman and her husband, Samuel, were introduced to Frank Lloyd Wright, and this led not only to the Freemans' textile block house in the Hollywood Hills, but the building of a community of designers, artists, actors, and musicians. The Freemans' house hosted a circle of friends including architect Rudolph Schindler and his wife, Pauline; Serbo-Croatian artist/decorator Gjura Stojano; Jean Negulesco, director of *How to Marry a Millionaire, Daddy Longlegs*, and *Titanic;* photographer Edward Weston; artist Margrethe Mather; dancer/choreographer Lester Hourton; art dealer Galka Scheyer (agent for Klee, Kandinsky, Feininger and Jawlensky ["the Blue Four"]); actor Albert Van Dekker and his wife, Esther; dancer Wyn Evans; and the Cuban Cocoanut Grove bandleader Xavier Cugat.

When Schindler arrived in Los Angeles in 1920, he had already been working with Wright since 1917, both in Chicago and at Taliesen East in Wisconsin. Schindler had come to America with the hope of teaming up with Wright since he was making what Schindler called "space architecture." As early as 1912 in Vienna, Schindler had declared in his architectural manifesto: "The architect has finally discovered the medium of his art: S P A C E. A new architectural problem has been born."[22] Schindler and his friend Richard Neutra both believed in a new conception of architecture as they had both trained in Vienna under the innovative concepts of Otto Wagner and Adolf Loos, and had been inspired by the Wasmuth publications of Frank Lloyd Wright's work, believing that America was the place for the new architecture.

The Barnsdall House, Los Angeles, 1920, designed by Frank Lloyd Wright. *Wayne Andrews*

However, in Schindler's earliest projects, the influence of the Moderne is visible. The 1922 duplexes he designed for a speculative investment project shows stepped decorative detail around the entrances that is Art Deco in style. And of the two 1929 houses Schindler built at Park Moderne in Calabasas for William Lingenbrink – one of Los Angeles' first patrons of the Moderne and the Modern style – the horizontal appearance of the projecting flat roofs and the narrow bands of clerestory windows lean toward the Streamline Moderne.

In 1925, Schindler was joined in Los Angeles by Neutra, who had stopped in New York and Chicago on his way from Vienna. Neutra and his wife, Dione, briefly moved into Schindler's Kings Road house – an experimental tilt-up concrete production – and they participated in the friendships that had spun off the Barnsdall project. In addition to the Freeman house meetings, the Schindlers' West Hollywood house became another meeting ground for the local cultural industry. Among the architects, designers, artists, poets, and writers who visited there were photographer Edward Weston, composer John Cage, reformer Theodore Dreiser, architect Lloyd Wright, and dancer John Bovington. Also attending their salons were Pauline Schindler's fellow teachers at the Barnsdall kindergarten, Harriet Press Freeman and her husband, Samuel, and Leah Press Lovell and her husband, Philip, who wrote a health column for the *Los Angeles Times*. The Lovells would soon commission a house both by Schindler at Newport Beach, 1926, and by Neutra in the Hollywood Hills, 1928-29.

Rudolph Schindler's design of a 1922 Duplex as shown in Sheldon Cheney's *New World Architecture*, 1930

Rudolph Schindler's design of a 1922 Duplex. *Elizabeth McMillian*

A detail of a Schindler design in the Los Feliz area shows the structural appearance of his repetitive ornament. *Elizabeth McMillian*

When Neutra arrived in Los Angeles in 1925, he and Schindler set up a partnership that they called Architectural Group for Industry and Commerce (AGIC). Few of their projects were built because most bankers and architectural boards considered modern architecture unattractive and unsaleable. Philip Lovell proposed his Neutra design as a "Demonstration Health House" to borrow money from his *Times* publisher Harry Chandler because no bank was interested in lending for the project.

After the house was finished and its *Times* publication still left Neutra without commissions, it was a disappointment to him to be considered simply an "experimenter." Shortly afterward, in 1931, Neutra and Schindler dissolved their partnership, although the two remained close in their moral commitment to modern architecture. However, the following year saw some glimmer of recognition for the two émigrés when one of AGIC's projects was included in the 1932 International Style show at New York's MOMA: Schindler and Neutra's 1927 Jardinette Apartments in Los Angeles. Neutra's design for the Lovell House, completed in 1929, was also included.

Neutra seized upon the opportunity and brought the show to Bullocks Wilshire, a Deco department store, completed in 1928-29. In an attempt to change bankers' and backers' position about the value of modern architecture, he invited the mayor, the governor, bank presidents, and the press, and asked the president of the University of Southern California to chair the host committee. Neutra's public relations gambit paid off: he was invited to conduct one of USC's graduate courses and received a commission for a house on Fishers Island, New York.

By the mid 1930s, the new modern architecture, like the popular Streamline style, began to gain some interest for its advertising value. Schindler's work reflected this style in his numerous commissions for transport companies, chic restaurants and retail shops, such as automobile showrooms for Maddux, Inc., an interior of a Lockheed model airplane, prototypes for Standard Oil Company and Union Oil Company gas stations, Sardi's Restaurant, and Brown, Smith & Moore, a café and restaurant for impresario Sid Grauman.

Living room interior of the Lovell House, Los Angeles, 1927, designed by Richard Neutra. *Girsberger*

However, it was Neutra's International Style put to commercial use that gained greater attention – and caused some to associate it with the Streamline style. By the mid-1930s, he had become the *avant-garde* architect of choice, designing stores, factories, schools, museums, airports, and an aluminum bus for White Motors Company. His fame became international since, in 1927, he had written a book in German about American building technology, *Wie Baut Amerika* (How America Builds), and thus was asked occasionally to be an international ambassador, writing articles in the international press, traveling for visiting lectures, and even proposing to CIAM that his small office become their first American chapter. Neutra's 1934-35 Beard House displays his tentative relationship to the Streamline Moderne style. He also designed homes for the *avant-garde* film community: for screenwriter Anita Loos, director Josef von Sternberg (a 1935 Streamline aluminum house subsequently owned by Ayn Rand and later demolished), writer/producer/director Albert Lewin, and actress Anna Sten and her husband, director Eugene Frenke. The Sten-Frenke home won *House Beautiful*'s modern house award in 1934, and by 1949, Neutra was so popular that he appeared on the cover of *Time* Magazine.

The Beard House, 1934-35, by Richard Neutra. *David Glomb*

A Streamline stair at the rear of the Beard House, 1934-35, by Richard Neutra. *David Glomb*

Spanning the 1930s and 1940s, another generation of modern architects built on the foundation laid by Gill, Wright, Neutra, and Schindler. Theoretically and formally following in his father's footsteps, Lloyd Wright was a part of this next generation. He already had been working in the Los Angeles area since the early 1920s, during which time he produced some innovative designs. Many had the decoratively patterned concrete textile blocks or patinated copper panels of his father's designs, which so easily associated both architects with the Moderne's Art Deco style. Lloyd Wright built houses for actress Jobyna Howland, actor Ramon Navarro and Navarro's business manager, Louis Samuel, as well as impresario John Sowden. The concrete textile-block house for Sowden, 1926, was centered around a stage-like courtyard that served as a backdrop for dramatic productions, musical performances, and films. Lloyd Wright's interest in scenographic design continued when he did set design for Paramount and two band shells for the Hollywood Bowl in 1927 and 1928. Earlier, he had assisted Gill in Torrance with planning and designing workers' homes and community buildings, and he also collaborated on public housing projects – the Ramona Gardens, 1939-40, and Aliso Village, 1941-43. There, he produced simple, unornamented rowhouses and apartment units where the main innovations were in site planning and landscape, in which he added parks and tree-lined walkways for pedestrian traffic.

Lloyd Wright designed three of Jake Zeitlin's bookshops in which the architecture sometimes drew more attention than the books. Humorously, Zeitlin later complained about this and that Wright's subtle, indirect lighting made bulbs so hard to replace that the shops got darker and darker. As a member of Zeitlin's circle, Wright participated in the culture industry of the region's intellectuals, along with émigré critic Louis Adamic, photographers Will Connell and Edward Weston, impresario Merle Armitage, artist Rockwell Kent, *Los Angeles Times* art editor Arthur Miller, critic-librarian Lawrence Clark Powell, opera singer Lawrence Tibbett, graphic designer Grace Marion Brown, and industrial designer Kem Weber. The group would also invite interesting visitors and newcomers.

Stage of the Hollywood Bowl, postcard, 1928 design by Lloyd Wright. *Tom Zimmerman Collection*

The Sowden House, Hollywood, 1926, designed by Lloyd Wright. The decorative textile-block entrance is now almost overgrown with vegetation. *Elizabeth McMillian*

View of the seating at the Hollywood Bowl, postcard, 1928 design by Lloyd Wright. *Tom Zimmerman Collection*

Opposite page:
The Samuels-Navarro House, Griffith Park, 1926-28, designed by Lloyd Wright. *Elizabeth McMillian*

The central portion of the façade of the Samuels-Navarro House, 1926-28, Lloyd Wright. *Elizabeth McMillian*

The Entenza House, Pacific Palisades, 1937, designed by Harwell Hamilton Harris. *Dapprich*

Harwell Hamilton Harris also participated in the next generation of work and developed a method for design based on an integral relationship with the landscape. Harris was from California; he was the grandson of a homesteader and the son of an architect-rancher from Redlands. After apprenticing with Neutra and Schindler, he was influenced by the gentler regional traditions of the Arts & Crafts bungalows of the Greene brothers, and Japanese art and architecture. He was also inspired by the modern spirit of the Synchromist paintings of Stanton Macdonald-Wright, with whom he had studied at the Art Students League. Harris' clients cared little about *avant-garde* trends and liked his work for its clear expression of the modern structure, primarily a simple one-room pavilion. For example, his own house is one large room – a wood framed pavilion with redwood posts and sliding screens, and structural elements external to the walls. The sliding walls and cantilevered floor joists allow the house to be balanced in, and participate with, the natural setting. In 1937, Harris built the Pacific Palisades house of *Arts & Architecture Magazine* publisher/editor John Entenza. It was a small, modern work, but the curved wall of the carport, a spiral staircase, and metal railing made it Streamline Moderne. This was Harris' only example of the style.

Having grown up with utopian socialist ideas, Gregory Ain was another member of the generation with Lloyd Wright and Harris. Ain's father was a founding member of the utopian Llano del Rio cooperative farming community in Antelope Valley and he had lived there in a tent as a child. Ain had become interested in modern architecture in 1925 when he was in high school and had visited Schindler's studio, and although he studied the modern traditions at USC, his socialist background left him with the desire to produce a practical modern architecture without artistic concerns. Several of Ain's clients sympathized with his socialist goals, such as bookseller Zeitlin and Rita and Max Lawrence, who founded Architectural Pottery. Ain wanted to produce a straightforward architecture that was designed so any carpenter could use it by employing conventional construction technologies. Some considered his work also a part of the stucco-box Streamline style since his work was that of the contractor-builder type that used efficient plans, economical construction, and few unnecessary details. He used wood-frame construction with a stucco finish, eliminating many costly elements and employing two-story, 4x4-inch posts, which also served as door and window jambs, such as seen at his Dunsmuir Flats, 1937.

In 1935, Ain produced a housing project for agricultural workers that was based on elements of the Buckminster Dymaxion House as well as Schindler's type of tilt-up concrete shelter. In 1940, he collaborated with Joseph Stein on the "One Family Defense House" made of precast concrete corner slabs, with plywood wall and roof panels, and employed the 4x4-inch posts typical of his earlier work.

Like Ain, Raphael Soriano also studied at USC and was concerned with economy and function more than stylistic effects. He was inspired by Neutra's modern style and his fascination with technology. Soriano's theory and work were in many ways similar to the early European modernists in that he preferred flat roofs, smooth stucco surfaces, glass walls and ribbon windows, and, on the interiors, he preferred built-in furniture and soffits with indirect light. Soriano's 1935 Lipetz House in Silverlake, however, leaned toward the Streamline. Its living room appeared like a ship's bridge with the use of metal for the horizontal windows and railings to add to the nautical feeling. After 1936, Soriano dropped the use of wood construction for the Lattisteel framing system after meeting its developer, Fritz Ruppell. This material and structural change freed him to produce long cantilevers and work in 4x20-foot modules.

Lloyd Wright, Harris, Ain, and Soriano – this second generation of modern architects – was fortunate that the influence of Roosevelt's PWA public buildings had given the public an interest in forms that were more abstract and geometric. There was the feeling of a new progressive aesthetic as popular architecture moved toward a stripped-down esthetic, as architects such as these balanced their formal rhetoric with their clients' needs. Most of their clients were middle-class families who were concerned with flexible, open plans and indoor-outdoor living, or commercial clients who wanted auto-oriented designs with cost-saving, industrial materials and technologies that had flexible planning for re-use and rentability.

Moderne Structuring of Architecture and Industrial Design

Again and again, some ultra-modern architects as influential as Wright, Schindler, Harris, Soriano, and Ain would adapt the 1920s Art Deco or the 1930s Streamline sensibility – or specific elements – to their work when it seemed appropriate to the commercial project or the house as the "machine for living," in Le Corbusier's terms. These architects were re-examining *structural* form and its relationship to utility and beauty, and the Moderne styles were effectively translated, not simply by decorative detail, but by the treatment of the structural elements.

Modern architect Douglas Honnold adopted the Art Deco flair for the house he designed with, and for, Metro Goldwyn Mayer's art director Cedric Gibbons. Gibbons, who designed the Academy Awards' Oscar, was married to actress Dolores del Rio, and their 1929 house has a formal Moderne feeling with linear decoration rather than the zigzags of the traditional Art Deco style. The double-height second-floor living room looked like one of MGM's great white sets of the same era and related it again to the "Perpendicular Style," as Art Deco was often called. Later, the work of another talented Los Angeles Modernist, Rodney Walker, would also blend Moderne with Modern structurally in his 1940 Lohrie House, with the extending and overlapping of horizontal planes and corner glass details.

In the 1930s, two Los Angeles modern architects, Erle Webster and Adrian Wilson, adopted the Streamline style for a Palm Springs vacation

The entrance of the Dolores Del Rio-Cedric Gibbons House, Pacific Palisades, 1929, designed by Douglas Honnold and Cedric Gibbons. *Tim Street-Porter*

The rear façade of the Dolores Del Rio-Cedric Gibbons House. *Tim Street-Porter*

house of a prominent Washington, D.C. family. Their 1936 Davidson House had such progressive streamlining, metal-railing, and curved glass walls perched on the edge of a mountain overlooking the desertscape that it has become known as the Ship of the Desert.

Particularly during Moderne's Streamline phase, it was the interest in suggesting, imitating, and exaggerating the *structural* details of everything from architecture to toasters that helped to popularize the role of the industrial designer during the same period. Furniture design and the applied arts were quickly changing to modern needs, materials, and production processes. Schindler had shown an interest in furniture design in which individual components would be made by machine but assembled by hand, and among the émigré community and its followers, the ideas of craftsmanship and quality were as hotly discussed in Los Angeles as they had been in Germany at the height of the Bauhaus School.

One émigré who preferred to call himself an industrial designer was Jock Detlof Peters, who came to Los Angeles in 1922. Peters gained his interest in the applied arts in Germany, where he had studied at a trade school and then worked from 1913 to 1914 in the office of Peter Behrens. Behrens was responsible for training a number of the leading Modern Movement architects. Walter Gropius, Mies van der Rohe, and Le Corbusier all worked in his office and, like Peters, acquired their interest in the industrial arts from Behrens.

The bulk of Peters' work in the 1920s shows what a masterful industrial designer and decorator he was. From 1924 to 1927, he was an art director for Famous Players/Lasky Films, during which time he designed the sets for *Road to Reno*, *This Is the Night*, *What Price Glory?* and stage sets for *Mars* and *The Mystery of Life*.

Peters continued to occasionally work for Lasky, but after 1927 he and his brother George established the Peters Brothers Modern American Design firm to design interiors and furnishings. They made carpet designs for Mohawk Mills and furniture for Universal Assembling Furniture. Some of their best Art Deco and Streamline work was done for store planners Feil and Paradise, who hired them to design Desmonds storefront, 1928, the Maddux Air Lines Building, 1928, and many of the interiors of the Art Deco department store Bullocks Wilshire, 1929.

Peters died at the peak of his career in 1934, but during the early '30s, he designed a number of houses. He collaborated with Schindler on the 1930-31 model houses and a community building for Willam Lingenbrink in Calabasas, in which he made use of the Moderne's strong vertical and horizontal structural contrasts. His Sheppard house in San Marino, 1934, features a large round Streamline window. However, his Gilks house in Hollywood, with its numerous balconies, is close to the Modern Movement designs of Neutra and Schindler from the same period.

Émigré J.R. Davidson first called himself an industrial designer, then later an architect. Before arriving in Los Angeles in 1925, he worked in London, Paris, Berlin, and New York. In London, he learned about ocean liner design, and in Paris, he learned about cubism and collage, rich materials and color. When he came to Los Angeles, he first worked for revival architect Robert D. Farquhar and designed movie sets for Gibbons and for director Cecil B. DeMille.

Davidson's commercial work of the '20s and early '30s drew on the glamour and glitz of Hollywood as he used new materials in new experimental ways, such as the façade for C.R. Hite that had chemically-stained green cement with aluminum trim, and rough-finished and lacquered bronze. Davidson used cadmium-plated steel and copper for the Hite-Bilike shops and copper with redwood on the Satyr Bookshop. After a fire destroyed Schindler's design of Sardi's Restaurant in 1936, Davidson finished the façade in blue and wine-red Carrara glass with a sidewalk of purple terrazzo. He also designed such trendy spots as the Nickabob Café and the Cocoanut Grove at the Ambassador Hotel.

Davidson followed the Moderne trend for decorative structural form in his storefront for Bari in Hollywood – a cubistic montage of solid and transparent stripes and rectangles. And he also oriented shopping to automobile traffic when he designed prototypes for drive-in markets where he treated the façades like they were window displays. By the mid-'30s and into the 1940s, he received more residential commissions. Both his Stothart (Phillips) house in Santa Monica, 1937-38, and his house for émigré writer Thomas Mann in Pacific Palisades, 1941, are functional, substantial and, unlike the Streamline bent of his commercial work, they followed more closely the tenets of the Modern Movement.

Industrial designer Kem Weber was a friend of Davidson's and also aided in shaping the commercial design aesthetic of Southern California in its store façades and interiors, and in its furniture and fixtures. The German-born Weber trained in his homeland in the applied arts, and when he moved to the United States in 1914, it was to work on the German exhibition at the Pan Pacific Exposition in San Francisco. After World War I broke out, Weber decided to stay in California and open a design studio in Santa Barbara. There he began to produce fixtures, furniture, and artwork, but was asked to join the design department of Barker Brothers in 1921. He worked there first as a draftsman and then as art director until 1927. While at Barker Brothers, Weber developed their modern lines and opened their Modes and Manners shop, which was the first modern retail outlet in Southern California. After 1927, when Weber again opened his own studio, he continued to work with Barker Brothers, creating their Tempo shop in 1934.

In 1927, Weber became an organizer of American Union of Decorative Artists and Craftsmen (AUDAC) and participated in their first exhibition in Brooklyn in 1931. His designs and his organizing skills in such organizations earned him the chairmanship of the first Department of Industrial Design at Art Center School during the same year and there he taught that marketing and sales were part of the success of creating good design.

The storefront of Desmonds Department Store, Los Angeles, 1928-29, designed by Jock Peters with Feil and Paradise. *Elizabeth McMillian*

Among Weber's furniture designs were lamps, silverware, clocks, silverware, his famous "Airline Chair," and tubular steel chairs and tables. Process was also important to him and his mass-produced Bentlock furniture was manufactured by the Ford assembly line method. It replaced mortise and tenon and dowel joints with a bent machine-made element that was reinforced with an oval lock of solid wood. With this method, the designer produced 125 different pieces – tables, chests of drawers, and cabinets – out of a few basic units. Weber did the interiors and a mural for Vultee Aircraft Corporation; the studio of photographer Will Connell, 1936; a roadside restaurant and gas station, developed with Art Center students, 1935; and numerous shops – Hartfield Hosiery, Kerr Sport Shop, Colburn's Fur Store, Zacho's Store, Hudson's Credit Jewelers, Roos Brother Shoe Store, Sommer and Kaufmann stores. In the 1930s, he also joined Jock Peters in creating sets for German art director Hans Drier at Paramount.

Weber designed some mildly Streamline Moderne houses in the late '30s, such as the Wedemeyer house in Altadena, 1937, and the Gisler house in Glendale, 1942-43, and also participated in designs for prefabrication for defense housing in World War II. However, Weber's most interesting work, and one which was the most cohesive project produced in Southern California prior to that war, was the design of Walt Disney's 51-acre animation studio in Burbank, 1939-40. It included planning, architecture, interior design, custom furniture and graphic design for offices, stages, restaurant, service station, penthouse, gym, and lounge.

Another who labeled himself an industrial designer and was a latecomer to the Los Angeles scene was Paul Laszlo. After arriving in the city in 1937, he became immersed in commercial interiors work and furniture design. His showroom on Rodeo Drive in Beverly Hills was a fashionable shopping spot for the upper middle-class. Lazlo also produced some Moderne residences that ranged between European Modern style and the Streamline Moderne with nautical touches. His own house was a bit more reserved with interiors that were quite luxurious and a version of what would be called posh Hollywood Moderne.

Swiss-born Albert Frey was another latecomer to the Moderne scene as he settled in Palm Springs in 1934. He advocated a pure functionalist aesthetic that he learned from his fellow countryman Le Corbusier for whom he had worked in Paris from 1928 until 1930. Frey wrote *In Search of a Living Architecture*, 1939, which affirmed his belief in technical progress over aesthetic appearances. Nonetheless, since Frey liked to work in aluminum and light steel and preferred to integrate his structures into the natural landscape, the contrast of nature and man-made structures were quite picturesque, especially in the desert setting of Palm Springs. There, Frey worked with John Porter Clark and completed homes and schools, churches, hospitals, and the City Hall.

The Airline Chair, 1934-45, designed by Kem Weber. *Santa Barbara Architectural Archive*

Furnishings and Art For The Moderne Styles

New York industrial designer Paul T. Frankl also moved to Los Angeles in the 1930s. He was famous for his "skyscraper furniture," sturdy wooden bookcases, cabinets, and desks designed in the late 1920s. Frankl's reputation was enhanced by his writing of a small book titled *Form and Reform*, 1930, which proclaimed the value of style. In his "Style versus Styles" chapter, he wrote, "What elevated men, in the last analysis, above the bees is the mastery and recognition of Style." Articles and books like his were popular with the middle class, but distrusted by purists of the Modern Movement. Frankl was joined in this populist sentiment by Sheldon Cheney and his wife, Martha, who had also moved to Los Angeles from the east coast. The Cheneys' *Art and the Machine,* 1936, stated, "We live in a world of Streamline vehicles....As an esthetic mark, and a symbol of the twentieth century machine-age speed, precision, and efficiency, it has been borrowed from the airplane and made to compel the eye anew...."[23]

Modern designers and modern clients following these trends wanted fine modern furniture and decorative products for their homes and offices. If they could afford them, they purchased furniture by Frankl, Weber, Laszlo, or Hendrick Van Kepel. Laszlo, Frankl, Maria Kipp, and Tilli Lorch also produced modern textiles, and craftsmen such as Otto and Gertrude Natzler, Glen Lukens, and Beatrice Wood designed modern ceramics. Company's like Rita and Max Lawrence's Architectural Pottery, Pacific Clay Products, and Gladding McBean produced innovative lines and even managed to *Moderne*-ize California's Spanish-Mexican past with colorful pots and tableware that had strong Deco outlines and vivid color.

Among Los Angeles' émigré craftspeople who added to the Moderne's progressive sense of style was master Austrian jeweler Adolph Feil. He first immigrated to the Oakland-San Francisco area in 1903, but moved to Southern California after the 1906 San Francisco fire. Feil's wealthy clientele led him to commissions from Fox Studios, where he produced the Art Deco Egyptian-style amulets, bracelets, anklets, rings, toe rings, headwear, and necklaces for Theda Bara in *Cleopatra*. His Moderne fame came with the design of the luxurious Ronson lighters and other smoking accessories that suited the posh Art Deco and Streamline interior.

Painting and sculpture were also essential to the well-furnished Moderne interior. In the 1920s, Los Angeles had seen the influx of international artistic talent and the establishment of the Group of Independent Artists of Los Angeles, who held their first exhibition in 1923. This group represented a critical current in local art that joined to support the new forms of Cubism, Dynamism, and Expressionism. They united against the landscape romantics, such as the Eucalyptus painters, Laguna seascape painters, and Mission painters, who perpetuated the idyllic myth of California. Leading the group were Synchromist painter Stanton Macdonald-Wright, who had come from Cubist Paris before World War I, and the radical Lithuanian exile Boris Deutsch. The Independents and other local talent were transformed by their encounter with the Mexican muralists. Diego Rivera, José Orozco, and José Siqueiros had visited Los Angeles in the 1930s. Orozco painted "Prometheus" at Pomona College, and Siqueiros taught at Chouinard Art Institute and painted an outdoor mural in the courtyard of the school. When given commissions, artists borrowed their stylistic mannerisms without the Marxist social content.

At work in Los Angeles were muralists Macdonald-Wright, Hugo Ballin, Millard Sheets, Herman Sachs, Anthony B. Heinsbergen, John Gabriel Beckman, Haldine Douglas, Ivan Bartlet and Jean Swiggett, Frank Bowers and Arthur Prunier, Edward Biberman, Buckley MacGurrin, Julian Ellsworth Garnsey, Fletcher Martin, Grace Clements, Maynard Dixon, Merrell Gage and Anna Katharine Skeele. Sculptors included Gjura Stojano, Salvatore Cartaino Scarpitto, George Stanley, Bartolo Mako, Nina Saemundsson, and Harold Wilson. Photomurals were gaining popularity as well and Will Connell and Edward Weston, among others, provided them for numerous offices, for example, Connell's murals for the offices of Columbia Steel Company.

These artists taught – or their works were known by the professors – at the local art schools: Otis Art Institute, Chouinard, University of California at Los Angeles, Occidental College, University of Southern California, the California Institute of Technology and Claremont College. With industrial designers, such as Weber, and photographers, such as Connell and Ansel Adams, at the Art Center School, it became one of the most professional arts and crafts schools in the country. All of these schools flourished with regional talent as well as gathering visiting designers and artists from around the world. New materials and new technologies were taught along with new concepts.

New York industrial designer Paul Frankl settled in Los Angeles in the 1930s. His furnishings in a New York apartment were published in Sheldon Cheney's popular *The New World Architecture*, 1930. Shortly after, Sheldon and Martha Cheney also moved to L.A. *Sheldon Cheney, The New World Architecture, 1930*

Left:
A Rudolph Schindler-designed chair reproduced by Marmol Radziner and Associates. *©2003 fotoworks-Benny Chan*

Opposite page, top:
Ships depicted in Herman Sachs' murals for Bullocks Wilshire Department Store, 1928-29. *Tom Zimmerman*

Opposite page, bottom:
Planes and a dirigible depicted in Sachs' murals for Bullocks Wilshire Department Store. *Tom Zimmerman*

MADDUX
GRAF ZEPPELIN
D-LZ 127

II. Deco Details and Streamline Structure

Art Deco Elements

Los Angeles' Art Deco style was identifiable by architectural ornament in two-dimensional, highly-decorative patterns of chevrons, spirals, and motifs borrowed from Gothic, Egyptian, Assyrian and Classical historic periods. Even the motifs borrowed from the natural world – such as plants and flowers, and elegantly silhouetted animals such as horses, deer and bulls – were carefully stylized to suit the entire architectural composition.

Since formal compositions were of primary concern, Art Deco buildings tended to be monumental and studied with balanced symmetrical elevations. On the main elevation, usually the front façade, this symmetry often accompanied a hierarchical pattern, with a stepped volumetric composition focused on a central tower. From commercial buildings to schools and even houses, Art Deco structures featured towers, whether diminutive or tall.

Windows and decorations were arranged in recessed vertical panels, leaving the surfaces of the structures in smooth form to emphasize the overall modern look created by smooth, progressive-appearing volumes. Adding to this sense of modern block-like volumes, the roofs were flat, but defined by a crown of simple or decorated parapets.

A detail of the tower on the 1930 commercial building designed by J.R. Horns at Poinsettia Place and Beverly Boulevard. *Elizabeth McMillian*

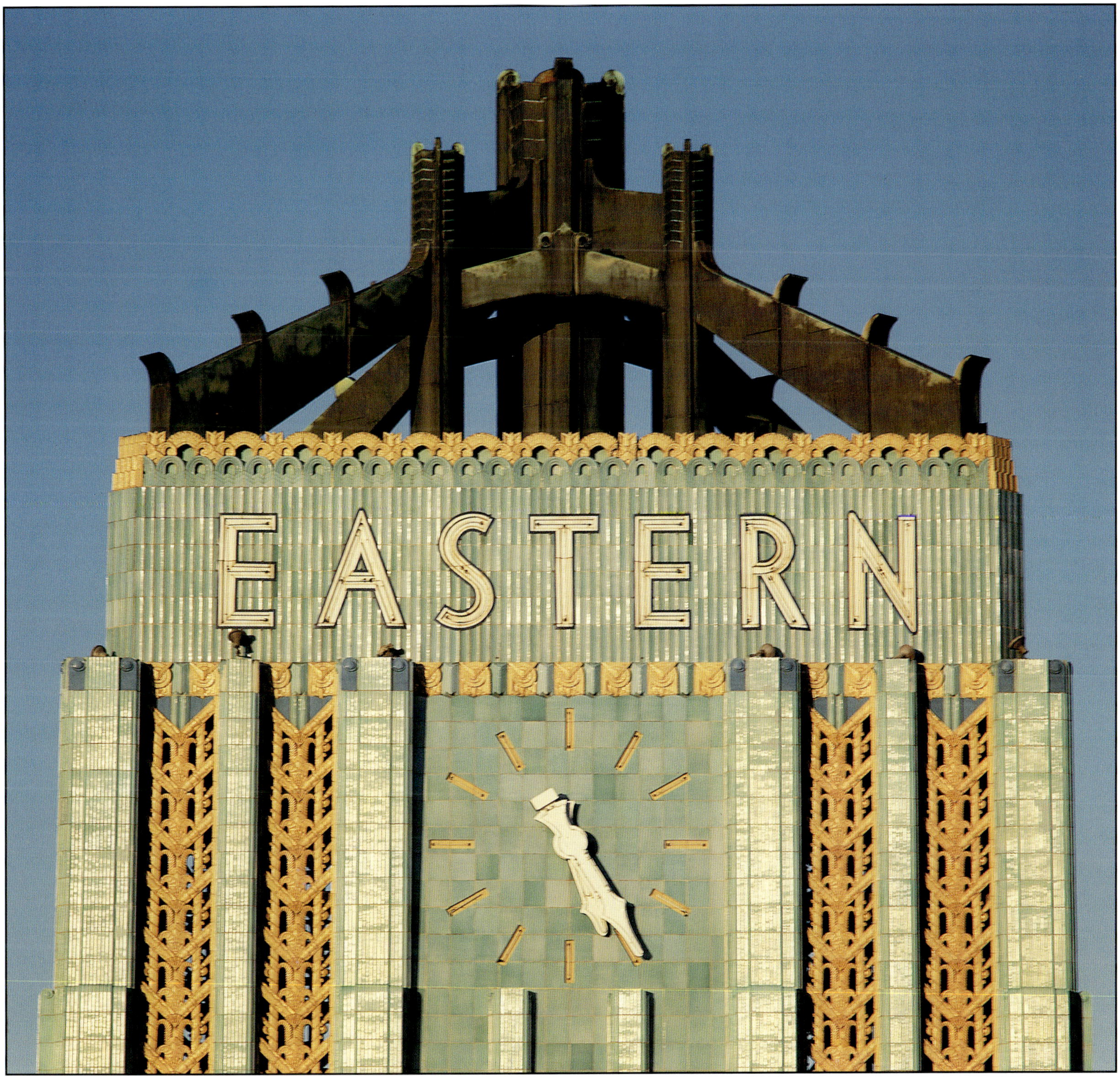

The top of the Eastern Building, 1930, designed by Claude Beelman. *Tom Zimmerman*

The Janus Gallery Building (now a gym and tanning facility), 1928. *Elizabeth McMillian*

Ornamental detail on the façade of Lloyd Wright's Samuels-Navarro house. *Elizabeth McMillian*

Theatre-designer S. Charles Lee's decorative ornament on his design of the MPA Office Building, 1928, southwest corner of Hollywood Boulevard and Western Avenue. *Elizabeth McMillian*

Sculptural ornament on the façade of the Sunset Tower (now the Argyle Hotel), 1929-31, designed by Leland A. Bryant. *Elizabeth McMillian*

EL REY
el Rey
EL REY
MATINEE
DAILY
12 NOON
GEO C SCOT
"MOVIE
MOVIE"

Opposite page:
A night view of the El Rey Theatre, circa 1928, designed by W. Cliff Balch. *Tom Zimmerman*

Sculptural detail along the roofline of the Pantages Theatre, 1929, designed by B. Marcus Priteca. *Elizabeth McMillian*

Sculptural ornament on the Owl Drug building, circa 1930, at the intersection of Wilshire and Roberston boulevards. *Elizabeth McMillian*

Details from the Wiltern Theatre-Pelissier Building, designed by Morgan, Walls & Clements with theatre design by Lansburgh and Heinsbergen, 1930-31. *Elizabeth McMillian*

Lloyd Wright's copper decorative trim on the 1926-28 Samuels-Navarro residence. *Elizabeth McMillian*

The two-story 5209 Wilshire Boulevard building is a black-and-gold terra-cotta structure in the style of the demolished Richfield Building. *Elizabeth McMillian*

Ornamental detail and a fresh color scheme enhance the Art Deco apartments on Echo Park. *Elizabeth McMillian*

Sculptural ornament on the Ravenswood Apartments located on Rossmore Street. *Elizabeth McMillian*

Chevron window details on the Sunset Tower (now the Argyle Hotel), 1929-31, designed by Leland A. Bryant. *Elizabeth McMillian*

Ornament at the rear garage entrance of the Sunset Tower (now the Argyle Hotel), 1929-31, designed by Leland A. Bryant. *Elizabeth McMillian*

Art Deco style stair risers at the entrance of a Malibu Art Deco-style guesthouse. © *2001 Renee M. Hadar, All Rights Reserved*

An Art Deco wall treatment at the Sunset Tower. *Elizabeth McMillian*

A pair of French Art Deco gates (attributed to Paul Kiss, c. 1920) which adorn a Malibu Art Deco-style guesthouse. © *2001 Renee M. Hadar, All Rights Reserved*

Spirals decorate a metal panel from the demolished Richfield Building, 1928. © *2001 Renee M. Hadar, All Rights Reserved*

Elevator door at the Garfield Building designed by Claude Beelman, 1928-29. *Elizabeth McMillian*

Lobby details of the Garfield Building in downtown Los Angeles. *Elizabeth McMillian*

More decorative lobby details of the 1928-29 Garfield Building. *Elizabeth McMillian*

Art Deco capital in the Wiltern Theatre designed by Lansburgh and Heinsbergen, 1930-31. *Elizabeth McMillian*

The fireplace mantle from the 1938 Michali Duplex. *Elizabeth McMillian*

Chandeliers and ceiling decoration of the Garfield Building designed by Claude Beelman, 1928-29. *Elizabeth McMillian*

Ceiling light in the lobby of the Sunset Tower (now the Argyle Hotel), 1929-31, designed by Leland A. Bryant. *Elizabeth McMillian*

An angular glass-and-metal Art Deco sconce.
© 2001 Renee M. Hadar, All Rights Reserved

Lalique glass table.
© 2001 Renee M. Hadar, All Rights Reserved

An Art Deco upholstered club chair. © *2001 Renee M. Hadar, All Rights Reserved*

A 1920s Art Deco chair with fan-patterned upholstery. © *2001 Renee M. Hadar, All Rights Reserved*

Swans' heads form the arms of a circa 1920s French Art Deco chair. © *2001 Renee M. Hadar, All Rights Reserved*

Streamline Elements

The Great Depression brought the end to Art Deco's lavish use of opulent materials, as building exteriors were stripped to sleek forms creating the ever-present *neutral white box*. The Streamline Moderne was identifiable by these stuccoed boxes, often multi-storied with rounded corners and curved projecting wings.

The Streamline Style saw traditional ornament discarded for the banding and accentuated curves of aerodynamic form that fascinated the industrial designers. Images from transport – trains, cars, airplanes, ships – and their materials – aluminum, chrome, plastics and steel – were used. Industrial-appearing glass-brick and ship-like pipe railing and porthole windows became popular.

These materials and images showed that the machine aesthetic of the Modern Movement's International Style was taken literally along with the intensified use of its flat roofs, smooth wall surfaces, ribbon windows, and glazed walls. Materials and forms emphasized the structure and simultaneously became its ornament.

The upper terrace of Milton J. Black's Streamline Mauritania Apartments, 1936. *Elizabeth McMillian*

A porthole window and banding are elements of a well-preserved Los Angeles Streamline apartment. *Elizabeth McMillian*

Banding accentuates the curves of a Milton J. Black apartment house on Kings Road. *Elizabeth McMillian*

Left:
Always ahead of his time like his father, Lloyd Wright designed Streamline front gates for the Art Deco-era Samuels-Navarro residence. *Elizabeth McMillian*

The rear gates of the 1926-28 Samuels-Navarro residence by Lloyd Wright. *Elizabeth McMillian*

The banding, curves and graphics of the entrance of the Thomas Jefferson High School. *Elizabeth McMillian*

One of the Streamlined entrance pylons that lead to the Hollywood Bowl. The 1935 sculptures were a federal arts project by George Stanley. *Tom Zimmerman*

The fountain and tiled outdoor seating of Milton J. Black's Mauritania Apartments, 1936. *Elizabeth McMillian*

Exterior stair at Richard Neutra's Beard House, 1934-35. *David Glomb*

A Streamline stainless steel torchere. *© 2001 Renee M. Hadar, All Rights Reserved*

The semicircular glass block stair of the Ulm House by William Kesling. *Elizabeth McMillian*

A striped pattern decorates an opaque glass door in the 1938 Michali Duplex. *Elizabeth McMillian*

The Streamline Style stair rail in the 1938 Michali Duplex. *Elizabeth McMillian*

A curved stair rail and concrete stairs in the Ulm House by William Kesling. *Elizabeth McMillian*

Window soffits in the Michali Duplex. *Elizabeth McMillian*

III. A Moderne City Survey[24]

Art Deco Style

The Art Deco style worked best for commercial buildings, theatres, public structures and schools, where its hierarchical formality provided status, unique identity, character, and prestige. Fewer individual houses were designed in the pure Deco style, since a casual vernacularism prevailed over the region's domestic works. Nonetheless, many period revival houses built in the late 1920s and 1930s were impacted in the execution of their details and ornament by the Art Deco style applied as a method of approach rather than a formal language. For instance, many a Spanish revival house or apartment building built under the Art Deco influence, known as SpanDeco, feature Spanish motifs ranging from spirals to tilework peacocks organized within zigzag parapets and lighted by chevron-pattered sconces. (One of the most prominent public examples of SpanDeco is Los Angeles' Union Passenger Terminal.) The same detailed influence was felt on Los Angeles' '30s production of English Gothic-, Italianate- and Regency-styled houses.

Art Deco Downtown

Starting with the downtown area, a number of the city's leading architects and firms – Claude Beelman; Morgan, Walls & Clements; A.C. Martin; Walker & Eisen; John & Donald B. Parkinson – all produced monumental Deco examples. While many have survived, the downtown's best commercial example unfortunately was demolished. It was the Richfield Building, the headquarters of the Richfield Oil Company, located at Sixth and Flower streets where it is now replaced by the twin ARCO Towers.

The 1928 Richfield Building, designed by Stiles O. Clements and the firm of Morgan, Walls & Clements, was an exceptional Deco building in its colors and materials. It was a twelve-story building sheathed in black, and trimmed in gold, terra-cotta. The trim was truly gilded in a fine coat of gold and it bolstered the claim that the building's appearance represented the company's wealth in "black gold."

A 130-foot tower, with a sign that spelled out RICHFIELD in neon, rose from the main volume of the building, which was created from a series of setbacks. Along the parapets of these setbacks, and at the main entrance, relief sculptures by Haig Patigian depicted stylized human figures and symbols of transportation – trains, planes and automobiles – which were fueled by the power of oil.

While it did not survive the modernization of downtown and outgrew its usefulness, the Richfield Building, built of steel-reinforced concrete, was among the first commercial structures in Los Angeles to provide two levels of underground parking.

Other downtown office buildings by Clements, with the firm of Morgan, Walls & Clements, include the Los Angeles Pacific Telephone Company Building, 1911, at 716 S. Olive Street, with a 1930 remodeling by the same firm that produced its Art Deco appearance, and enhanced by Timothy Walker & Associates, who renovated it in 1979 to make it appear more stylishly Art Deco. In 1916, the firm constructed the building and garage at the southwest corner of Broadway and Sixth Street, and later renovated both structures in 1934. The original was a Beaux Arts construction of stacked volumes in white terra-cotta with an upper arcade and broad projecting cornice incorporating later Art Deco flourishes such as the elegant entrance gates to the garage on Sixth Street.

Claude Beelman was perhaps the most prolific architect of the era working in the Art Deco style. In the downtown area alone, he was responsible for some of the best remaining Art Deco office and commercial buildings. The earliest was his L. Harris Realty Company (now the Los Angeles Fur Mart Building) at 635 S. Hill Street, done under the firm of Curlett & Beelman in 1925. The project combined Gothic details with Art Deco massing and setbacks. The exterior of the eight-story brick structure, clad in beige-colored terra-cotta, consists of five bays which step back in three levels. Continuous piers frame the bays of the lower three floors. Although its lobby and street level façade were altered, the design of the upper stories is original and consists of recessed window bays separated by metal spandrels between stories, culminating in segmented arches. The fourth through seventh stories are set back and united by continuous piers. The seventh-floor window heads have pointed arches over Gothic-influenced niches.

At 408 W. Eighth Street at Hill Street is Beelman's Garfield Building, 1928-29. This mature Art Deco design is #121 of Los Angeles Historic-Cultural Monuments and also listed on the National Register of Historic Places. Built for the Sun Realty Company, it is a twelve-story structure that combines Art Deco geometry with the organic swirls of the Art Nouveau style. The cream terra-cotta-clad exterior steps back at the third floor to create the U-plan of the upper stories. Crowning the building is a small, square tower. Stylized floral reliefs accent the spandrels in the vertical window strips, while sun patterns grace the lower stories. The main entrance is marked by an elaborate wrought-iron entrance canopy. Its underside is inlaid with a bright marble sunburst that echoes the terrazzo sidewalk below. Floral and grapevine patterns decorate the open grillwork above the entrance. On the inside, the lobby features walls and floors of alternating bands of black and purple antique marble. The 20-foot-tall lobby ceiling has a low-bas relief pattern in plaster and from it hang Gothic-style chandeliers in tones of gold and silver. The room is enhanced with polished Benedict nickel fittings and detailing in German silver and gold leaf for the elevator door and elegant display cases.

A two-story entrance is the most distinctive feature of Beelman's 1930 Ninth and Broadway Building, at 850 S. Broadway. Heavy piers capped by a segmented arch articulate the recessed entry. Above the entrance doors, a second segmented arch serves as the base for a vertical panel of terra-cotta ornament in a lush grapevine design. The body of this 13-story, steel-reinforced concrete office building is sheathed with tan-colored terra-cotta textured to resemble stone. The massing rises vertically with only a few shallow setbacks near the roofline. The attic level of the building also has a slight series of setbacks with panels of grapevine designs set between the piers. Metal spandrels between the recessed strips of windows employ an abstract geometric design. The remodeled lobby still retains the original elevator doors and cabs.

Opposite page:
The Richfield Building, Los Angeles, 1928, designed by Stiles O. Clements of Morgan, Walls & Clements. *Tom Zimmerman Collection*

RICHFIELD
HAVENSTRITE BUILDING
GATES HOTEL
HOTEL CLINTON
ROOMS

Entrance of the Richfield Building, Los Angeles, 1928. *Tom Zimmerman Collection*

The Richfield Building's date plaque with symbols of transportation, industry and commerce fueled by oil. *Tom Zimmerman Collection*

Beelman's Eastern Columbia Building (now the 849 Building), 1930, at 849 S. Broadway has assumed the mantle as Los Angeles' major Art Deco skyscraper since the 1972-73 demise of the Richfield Building. It is #294 of Los Angeles Historic-Cultural Monuments and opened as the new headquarters for both Eastern Outfitting Company, which sold home furnishings and appliances, and the Columbia Outfitting Company, which sold clothing and accessories. It is striking for its turquoise terra-cotta cladding and the four stylized flying buttresses that surround its central four-sided clock tower. The building is thirteen stories tall and built of steel and reinforced concrete. The turquoise terra-cotta is trimmed with deep blue and gold terra-cotta.

Emphasis on the building's vertical members is accentuated by deeply recessed bands of paired metal sash windows and spandrels with copper panels sporting stylized plant motifs. The terra-cotta is decorated with a wealth of motifs – sunburst patterns, geometric shapes, zigzags, chevrons and stylized animal- and plant-forms. The building sets back at the tenth, eleventh, and twelfth floors. The sidewalks surrounding the Broadway and Ninth Street sides are surfaced with multi-colored terrazzo in zigzag and chevron patterns.

The central main entrance features a recessed two-story lobby finished with a blue-and-gold terra-cotta sunburst. Before 1980, the lobby led to a pedestrian retail arcade running through the center of the building, defining one side of the structure as occupied by the Columbia Outfitting Company and the other by the Eastern Outfitting Company. In 1956, the owner's son closed the family retail business, but remodeled the Eastern Columbia Building for office space, and in the 1980s, the building was again refurbished and the lobby floor modified.

Beelman's turquoise terra-cotta Sun Realty Building (now Los Angeles Jewelry Center) at 629 S. Hill Street, was completed in 1930-31. A February 2, 1930 article in the *Los Angeles Times* announced that the soon-to-be-constructed Sun Realty Building would "follow the modern trend of architecture with an exterior of colored terra-cotta." Fluted turquoise terra-cotta piers rise, Gothic-style, fourteen stories to the roofline and taper to a crown of bronze ornament. The recessed panels between the piers define the building's metal sash windows that alternate with bronze spandrels covered with stylized patterns. At the fourth floor, the central façade is set back one bay, providing light and air circulation. In a 1970s remodeling, the lobby's marble floor and decorative plaster ceiling were removed; however, a few original fittings remain, including the original Art Deco elevator doors and rear entrance door with their abstract nature scenes.

EASTERN
EASTERN
First Interstate

Opposite page:
The Eastern Building, 1930, designed by Claude Beelman. *Tom Zimmerman*

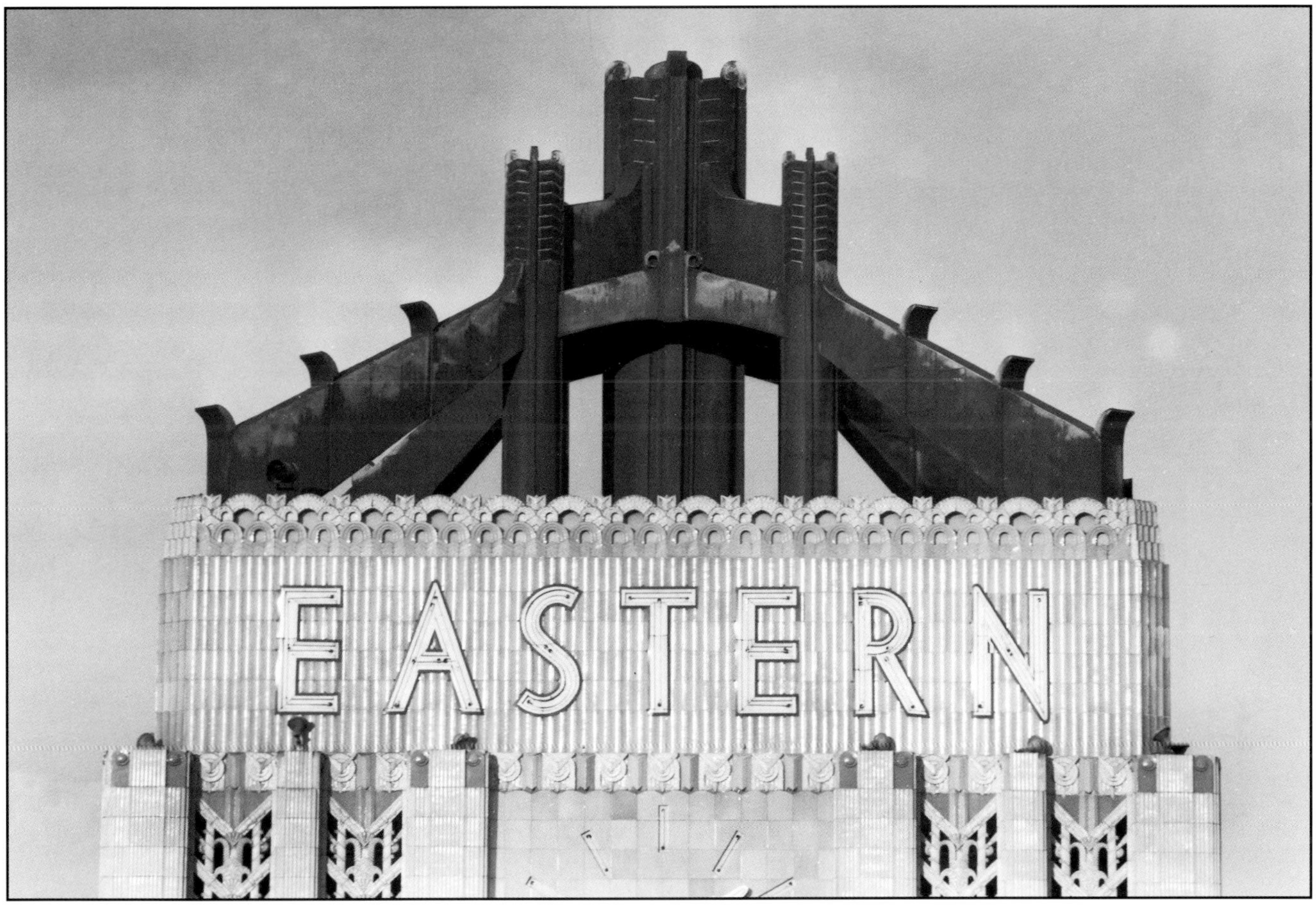

The neon sign and buttressing that crowns the tower of the Eastern Building, 1930, designed by Claude Beelman. *Tom Zimmerman*

Stylized buttresses crown the tower of the Eastern Building, 1930, designed by Claude Beelman. *Tom Zimmerman*

The renowned firm of father and son John & Donald B. Parkinson designed the 1929-31 Title Guarantee & Trust Building (also called the Guarantee Trust and now called the Four Eleven Building for its address at 411 W. Fifth Street), located at the northwest corner of Hill and Fifth streets. The twelve-story Art Deco skyscraper is sheathed in light buff terra cotta with a granite base. As #278 of Los Angeles Historic-Cultural Monuments and listed on the National Register of Historic Places, this building is one of the best Art Deco skyscrapers in the city. Architects John and Donald Parkinson followed the trend set by Hood's much-publicized 1926 Chicago Tribune Tower. In addition to the tower's Gothic verticality, parapets and flying buttresses, it includes heraldic shields and gargoyle-shaped drain spouts. The structure's verticality was accentuated at night by dramatic exterior lighting. Piers surround the recessed windows, emphasizing the height of the structure and extending above the roofline to create a parapet effect. Everything above the twelfth floor is unoccupied space, a design feature that allowed the building to extend beyond the 150-foot height limit in effect at the time of construction.

The interior elevator lobby is decorated with six murals by Hugo Ballin celebrating the Treaty of Cahuenga and various phases of Southern California history. Beginning with the earliest age in which sabertooth cats are shown at the La Brea Tar Pits, another panel illustrates the 1876 arrival of the railroad, while the modern-times panel depicts Los Angeles' rise to power through images of the Owens Valley aqueduct, oil derricks, machinery and, of course, an image of the very building, the Title Guarantee & Trust. (The Parkinsons' Banks-Huntley Building, 1929-31, at 632 Spring, is another example of an Art Deco skyscraper, and in this case, featuring a tower crowned with vertical chevron panels.)

Another downtown Art Deco office building worth noting is the William Fox Building, 1930-32, designed by S. Tilden Norton and located at 608 S. Hill Street. This building was the home base of Fox's empire that included over 1,100 movie palaces, and it was part of a complex which included the adjoining Los Angeles Theater that faces Broadway. The 13-story reinforced concrete building rises uninterrupted by the typical Art Deco setbacks and its façade is made of off-white terra-cotta with mauve tile spandrels decorated with chevrons and shields between the recessed windows. The original entrance remains intact. The opening contains a bronze-framed triple doorway and transom recessed beneath a flattened arch entrance. Geometric designs embellish the brass frames around the glass doors and cast stone floral moldings accent the doorway. The lobby is richly finished in green and purple marble bands and its elevators are topped by stylized bronze eagles.

Opposite page:
The Title Guarantee & Trust Building, 1929-31, designed by John & Donald B. Parkinson. *Tom Zimmerman*

Right:
Sculptural relief on the façade of the Title Guarantee & Trust Building. *Tom Zimmerman*

Thrifty

An interior lobby view of the Title Guarantee & Trust Building showing the chandelier and one mural by Hugo Ballin. *Tom Zimmerman*

A detail of one of the murals in the Title Guarantee & Trust lobby. *Tom Zimmerman*

The Southern California Edison Building (now One Bunker Hill), 1930-31, by Allison & Allison (Austin Whittlesey), at 601 W. Fifth Street (located at the northwest corner of S. Grand Avenue and Fifth Street) appears like a classical fourteen-story tower. However, the deep-cut vertical window units and the ornament inside and out – a cubic pattern – is definitely Art Deco. The three-story base is limestone and the upper stories and tower are clad with buff-colored terra-cotta. The building steps back to a decorative tower that originally was lit with a neon sign spelling out EDISON. In the two-story lobby, classical elements are treated with an Art Deco manner. The building is #347 of Los Angeles Historic-Cultural Monuments, and as the office of a utility company, the building was one of the first electrically heated and cooled buildings built in the western United States. Its decorative program expresses the symbolic values of electric power: Over the octagonal entrance are allegorical figures representing hydroelectric energy, light and power, by sculptor Merrell Gage, and at the elevator lobby is a mural titled *Apotheosis of Power* by Hugo Ballin.

The firm of Walker & Eisen had worked in downtown L.A. and in 1928 designed the Art Deco-style Title Insurance and Trust Company Building (now the Los Angeles Design Center), at 433 S. Spring Street. Their reserved Art Deco design was far more enriched on the interior. They hired painter-muralist Ballin to design the entrance mosaic panels and murals, and brought in Herman Sachs to decorate the lobby and its elevator doors. Walker & Eisen showed a flair for incorporating the current architectural trends and rich artistic embellishments.

The Southern California Edison Building (now One Bunker Hill), 1930-31, designed by Austin Whittlesey of Allison & Allison. *Tom Zimmerman*

Merrell Gage's allegorical relief sculpture on the façade of the Edison Building. *Tom Zimmerman*

Right:
The lobby of the Edison Building. *Tom Zimmerman*

A detail of the lobby ceiling of the Edison Building. *Tom Zimmerman*

Title Insurance and Trust Company Building, 1928, designed by Walker & Eisen. *Tom Zimmerman*

Lobby ceiling of the Title Insurance Building. *Tom Zimmerman*

Rear lobby of the Title Insurance Building. *Tom Zimmerman*

Ornament decorating one of the elevators of the 1928 Title Insurance Building. *Tom Zimmerman*

An original interior of the 1928 Title Insurance Building shows Art Deco furnishings and large murals by Herman Sachs. *California State Library*

Downtown Art Deco Stores

Walker & Eisen's design for the Oviatt Building at 617 S. Olive Street celebrates the best of the Art Deco spirit for store design and is now #195 of Los Angeles Historic-Cultural Monuments. This building was constructed as the headquarters for one of the most prestigious haberdasheries in the city, Alexander & Oviatt. It also housed rentable office space and a penthouse suite for owner James Oviatt and his wife.

First designed as an Italian Romanesque tower, the building was halted in the early stages of construction. The design was brought back to the drawing board after Oviatt attended the 1925 Paris Exposition and decided to decorate his building in the new Moderne style. The final work is still Romanesque in formal imagery, but Art Deco in execution.

Originally, the lobby forecourt contained over thirty tons of glass by French designer René Lalique, and a few original pieces remain in the panels at the top of the lobby columns. Lalique also designed the metalwork for the elevator doors, mailboxes, and directories. (The Art Deco-style iron

The upper stories of the 1927-28 Oviatt Building designed by Walker & Eisen. *Tom Zimmerman*

gates at the entrance were added in 1976 when the building was restored and modified as a restaurant and office building by Brenda Levin Associates.) The shop interior (now a restaurant) retains the Art Deco fixtures, stairs rails, and molded plaster ceiling panels.

Publications of the time described the building as "Ultra Modern," explaining that the shop front, marquee and interior decorative work were designed and produced in France and shipped to Los Angeles, along with five French engineers and architects to supervise the installation. Mr. Oviatt also hired the Parisian firm of Saddier et Fils to decorate his sophisticated ten-room penthouse with Art Deco furnishings and decorative arts. The rooms have survived and feature burled mahogany furniture and cabinets, parquet wood floors, carved woodwork, imported fabrics, and Lalique glass. Outside, the roof terrace once held gardens, a putting green, tennis courts, a swimming pool and a sandy beach with potted palms, but it is still an excellent place to view the clock tower lit by neon in the evening.

Lighted, faceted Lalique panels lit the original storefront of the 1927-28 Alexander & Oviatt store (referred to as the Oviatt Building). *Tom Zimmerman Collection*

The store entrance of the Oviatt Building as it appeared after renovation for use as a restaurant. The Art Deco-style gates are not original to the building. *Tom Zimmerman*

A corner and signage of the 1927-28 Oviatt Building. *Tom Zimmerman*

The clock tower above the Oviatt Building. *Tom Zimmerman*

A spire on the roof deck of the Oviatt Building provided a folly for visitors to the penthouse. *Tom Zimmerman*

The Oviatt Building as it appears today. *Elizabeth McMillian*

Opposite page: The fireplace in the living room of the Oviatt penthouse. *Elizabeth McMillian*

The entrance to the Oviatt penthouse decorated by the Parisian firm of Saddier et Fils. *Elizabeth McMillian*

A mural decorates the dining room of the Oviatt penthouse. *Elizabeth McMillian*

Right:
The hallway of the Oviatt penthouse features a sculpture of Mercury and photographs of the Oviatts' visiting celebrities and friends. *Elizabeth McMillian*

Opposite page:
An exotic bar for serving parties in the Oviatt penthouse. *Elizabeth McMillian*

Opposite page:
A small terrace opens to the bedroom of the Oviatt penthouse. *Elizabeth McMillian*

The master bath of the Oviatt penthouse. *Tom Zimmerman*

The shower of the Oviatt penthouse master bath shows the relief treatment of the walls. *Tom Zimmerman*

Outside the downtown area, scores of savvy merchants adopted the Art Deco style for its flashy sales potential. The most notable was the Bullocks Wilshire Department Store, located west of MacArthur Park on Wilshire Boulevard, extending the commercial district westward through the rich suburbs. It was designed in 1928-29 by architects John & Donald B. Parkinson with interiors by Feil and Paradise, who hired Jock Peters as architect-designer of the interiors. The store's owner, P.G. Winnett, also visited the 1925 Paris exposition, and like James Oviatt, he came back with ideas to embellish his new department store with an assortment of Moderne ideas. The picturesquely stepped and towered structure was sheathed in light terra-cotta panels from Gladding McBean and trimmed with weathered green copper. It was only five stories tall and was meant to be the first phase of a ten-story structure. Its main entrance feature was a large port cochere facing to the east side of the building and to the parking lot. This breezeway entrance was decked out with uniformed parking valets, potted palms and a rich ceiling mural by Herman Sachs, depicting modes of contemporary travel.

Much remains of the store's Art Deco interior design, although the building suffered some damage in the 1992 riots and was closed in 1993. (It is now owned by Southwestern University School of Law and functions as a library.) What is interesting about Peters' interior design is that not all departments were Art Deco-inspired, but drew very superficially on other aspects of the Modern Movement to suit the theme of the department. The menswear section was finished to appear like one of Frank Lloyd Wright's rugged concrete block designs, and other sections drew on cubist Bauhaus volumes, like the Saddle Shop and the infant wear department with its open mezzanine. Peters employed well-known émigré artists to decorate walls and panels, like the relief sculpture entitled *The Spirit of Sports* by Gjura Stojano for the walls of the sports shop. Other modern decorations were by Mayer Krieg, John Weaver and David Collins, and there were also traditional murals by George De Winter in the period-style fur department.

Below:
Bullocks Wilshire Department Store. A 1930s view of the 1928-29 tower structure designed by John & Donald B. Parkinson with interiors by Jock Peters with Feil and Paradise. *Tom Zimmerman Collection*

Opposite page:
A night-view 1930s postcard of Bullocks Wilshire Department Store. *Tom Zimmerman Collection*

BULLOCK'S
WILSHIRE

The 1928-29 Bullocks Wilshire Department Store. *Tom Zimmerman*

A Herman Sachs mural – depicting the god of Mercury – decorates the skylit porte cochere entrance to Bullocks Wilshire. *Tom Zimmerman*

The parking entrance gate to Bullocks Wilshire. *Tom Zimmerman*

Bullocks Wilshire's distinctive signage. *Tom Zimmerman*

Desmonds, 1928-29, designed by Gilbert Stanley Underwood. (Jock Peters and Feil and Paradise collaborated with Underwood, and Peters is responsible for the storefront.) *Elizabeth McMillian*

Other Art Deco Commercial Buildings and Office Towers

Desmonds, 1928-29, Gilbert Stanley Underwood, 5514 Wilshire Boulevard. (Jock Peters and Feil and Paradise collaborated with Underwood, and Peters is responsible for the storefront.)

The Selig Retail Store Building, 1931, Arthur E. Harvey, northwest corner of Western Avenue and Third Street. (This is a small black and gold building designed in the manner of the Richfield Building.)

Carl's Supermarket Building, 1933, Morgan, Walls & Clements, 1532-36 W. Sixth Street.

Retail Shop, circa 1930, 153 La Brea Avenue.

Owl Drug Store Building, circa 1930, southwest corner of Wilshire and Robertson boulevards.

The Kress and Company Building (now Frederick's), 1935, Edward F. Sibbert, located at 6606-12 Hollywood Boulevard. (Sibbert is the New York-based architect who designed all of the Kress stores.)

J.J. Newbury Company Building, 1928, 6600-04 Hollywood Boulevard.

Commercial Building, circa 1928, 9441 Wilshire Boulevard, Beverly Hills.

Pennsylvania Oil and Tire Warehouse, 1930, Bennett & Haskell, 33 Delacey Avenue, Pasadena.

Royal Laundry Building, 1927, with addition from circa 1935, Gordon B. Kaufmann, 443 S. Raymond Street, Pasadena.

Two Retail Commercial Buildings, circa 1934, 4500 block of W. Adams, north of Wellington Road.

Retail Store Building, 1930, 312-316 Elm Avenue, Long Beach.

Hancock Motors, 1929, Schilling & Schilling, southeast corner of Anaheim and Linden streets, Long Beach.

Pacific Auto Works, 1928-29, Schilling & Schilling, 1910 Long Beach Boulevard, Long Beach.

Auto Parts Shop, circa 1930, northeast corner of San Antonio Drive and Sproul Street, Norwalk.

Retail Store Building, circa 1932, 53 Huntington Drive, Arcadia. (The relief sculpture is by J.J. Mora.)

Dominguez-Wilshire Building, 1930, Morgan, Walls & Clements, 5410 Wilshire Boulevard.

Opposite page:
The Dominguez-Wilshire Building, 1930, designed by Morgan, Walls & Clements. *Elizabeth McMillian*

Wilshire
EXPRESS
익스프레스
OPEN

A corner detail of the Dominguez-Wilshire Building. *Elizabeth McMillian*

Decorative detail at the entrance to the Dominguez-Wilshire Building. *Elizabeth McMillian*

The entrance of the Dominguez-Wilshire Building. *Elizabeth McMillian*

Wilson Building, 1929, architects Meyer & Holler, northeast corner of Wilshire Boulevard and La Brea Avenue.

Office Building, 1936, Walker & Eisen, northwest corner of Wilshire Boulevard and Alexandria Street.

Wilshire Professional Building, 1929, Arthur E. Harvey, 3875 Wilshire Boulevard.

Commercial Bldg, 1927, Frank M. Tyler, 5464 Wilshire Boulevard.

MPA Office Building, 1928, S. Charles Lee, southwest corner of Hollywood Boulevard and Western Avenue.

United California Bank (now Bank Theater Building), 1929, Bennett & Haskell, northeast corner of N. Raymond and E. Colorado streets, Pasadena.

Warner Building, 1927, Marston and Maybury with designer Jess Stanton, 481 E. Colorado Boulevard.

American Storage Company Building, 1928-9, Arthur E. Harvey, 3639 Beverly Boulevard.

Commercial Building, 1930, J.R. Horns, southeast corner of Poinsettia Place and Beverly Boulevard.

Commercial Building, 1929, L. Mulgreen, 7223 Beverly Boulevard.

Parking Garage Building, circa 1926, 824 Western Avenue.

Janus Gallery, circa 1928, northwest corner of Beverly Boulevard and Sweetzer Avenue.

Shane Building, 1930, S. Norton, F. Wallis, 6652-6654 Hollywood Boulevard.

Yucca-Vine Tower Building, circa 1928, Gogerty & Weyl, northwest corner of Yucca and Vine.

Producers Film Center, circa 1928, architect unknown, located at the southeast corner of Romaine Street and Sycamore Avenue.

Bay City Guaranty & Loan Association Building, 1929-30, Walker & Eisen, 1225 Santa Monica Mall.

Central Tower Building, 1929, Eugene Durfee, 1424 Seventh Street, Santa Monica.

Rowan Building (Bradley Building), 1930, northwest corner of Pine Street and Broadway, Long Beach.

Citizen Publishing and Printing Company Building, 1929, 9355 Washington Boulevard, Baldwin Hills.

Lafayette Hotel Building, 1929, Schilling & Schilling, southwest corner of Broadway and Linden Street, Long Beach.

New Robinson Hotel, 1933-34, 334 E. Ocean Boulevard, Long Beach.

The Janus Gallery Building (now a sports and tanning facility), 1928. *Elizabeth McMillian*

Art Deco Store, 1929, at 7221 Beverly Boulevard, designed by L. Mulgreen. *Elizabeth McMillian*

Art Deco Theatres

The stylized decorative excess and commercial appeal of the Art Deco style suited cinema design. A number of leading architects received commissions for these special projects, particularly the firm of Morgan, Walls & Clements, G. Albert Lansburgh and Anthony B. Heinsbergen, and Seattle-based B. Marcus Priteca. Famed theater-designer S. Charles Lee designed the exuberant Fox Wilshire Theater, 1929, in West Hollywood, at 8440 Wilshire Boulevard, which fits within the Art Deco category, but Lee continued into the next decade to create several Streamline Moderne theatres. Also, Art Deco exoticism produced some of the most memorable movie palaces built anywhere in the world in the 1920s and '30s. Particularly notable are Grauman's Chinese, by Meyer & Holler, in 1927, at 6925 Hollywood Boulevard, and the Egyptian Theater, 1922, also by Meyer & Holler, at 6712 Hollywood Boulevard.

One of the most stunning Art Deco interiors was created by B. Marcus Priteca for the 1929 Pantages Theater Building located at 6233 Hollywood Boulevard. The theatre features a rich forecourt, lobby with grand symmetrical staircases, and a gilded, bedecked auditorium. Howard Hughes bought the theatre in 1949 and for a decade after the theatre hosted the Academy Awards. Since 1977, it has been used for live theatrical productions.

In San Pedro, the Fox-Warner Brothers Theater, 1931, located at 478 W. Sixth Street by L.A. Smith with theater designers Priteca and Heinsbergen, is modestly sized to suit the San Pedro neighborhood scale. When it opened on January 20, 1931, it was the first theater in the South Bay to be equipped with sound. Today the Art Deco theatre has been restored and is a key component of San Pedro's civic center. Two other Art Deco theatres by Priteca are the Pacific Theatre, 1931, at 9404 Wilshire Boulevard in Beverly Hills (which is Art Deco with a Mexican accent), and the Warner Brothers Theater, 1930, located at 6714 S. Pacific Boulevard in Huntington Park.

The Mid-Wilshire area features the Warner Brothers Western Theater, now known as the Wiltern Theater, and part of a complex with the Pellissier Building that is located at 3790 Wilshire Boulevard at Western Avenue. The Wiltern and its complex were designed by Morgan, Walls & Clements in 1930-31, with theater design by Lansburgh and Heinsbergen. Designed by Stiles O. Clements as a turquoise terra-cotta Art Deco building, it houses an office tower, the theatre, and two retail wings that spread out to either side of the theater entrance. From a distance, the twelve-story Pellissier office tower appears like a taller building because the narrowness of the vertical recessed band windows and spandrels remove any reference to scale. The 2,433-seat former Warner Brothers Western Theatre was Lansburgh's last major theater design and it remains intact following a $4.5-million 1985 restoration by Brenda Levin Associates for developer Wayne Ratkovitch.

On Santa Catalina Island, William Wrigley employed Weber and Spaulding to design the Avalon, a grand casino featuring motion pictures on the first floor and a ballroom on the second. The exterior is a mixture of Spanish, Moorish, and Art Deco styles with the circular volume extending out to the sea. The ground floor (bay side) houses the headquarters and museum of the Catalina Island Museum Society. The nine Art Deco nautical murals decorating the entrance loggia are by John Gabriel Beckman, whose commissions included Grauman's Chinese. The casino's 1,200-seat theatre was the first theatre engineered for sound and is so acoustically fine that the engineers of Radio City Music Hall studied it in 1931. Its only changes have been the additions of a 1949 refreshment stand and a 1953 Cinemascope screen. During World War II, the Avalon became a classroom for seamen and a USO center presenting Bob Hope, Kate Smith and Spike Jones. When they shot on and around Catalina Island, Hollywood heavies Cecil B. DeMille, Louis B. Mayer, John Ford and Erich von Stroheim used the Avalon to view their daily rushes.

The Wiltern Theatre-Pelissier Building, designed by Morgan, Walls & Clements with theatre design by Lansburgh and Heinsbergen, 1930-31. *Elizabeth McMillian*

Exterior detail of the Wiltern Theatre-Pelissier Building. *Elizabeth McMillian*

The mezzanine and lobby ceiling of the 1930-31 Wiltern Theatre designed by G. Albert Lansburgh and muralist Anthony B. Heinsbergen. *Elizabeth McMillian*

Interior detail of wall ornament and indirect lighting at the 1930-31 Wiltern Theatre designed by G. Albert Lansburgh and renovated by Brenda A. Levin and Maureen Sullivan in 1986. *Elizabeth McMillian*

The Roxie Theater, 1932, John M. Cooper. *Tom Zimmerman*

Other Art Deco Theatres

Roxie Theater, 1932, John M. Cooper, 518 S. Broadway, Los Angeles.

Warner Theater Building (now Pacific Hollywood), 1926-27, G. Albert Lansburgh, 6423-6445 Hollywood Boulevard.

Leimert Theater (now Jehovah Witness Hall), 1931-32, Morgan, Walls & Clements, 3300 Forty-third Place.

El Rey Theater, circa 1928, W. Cliff Balch, 5519 Wilshire Boulevard.

Belmont Theater Building, 1929, Reginald R. Inwood, southeast corner of St. Joseph Avenue and Second Street, Belmont Shores.

Fox Westwood Village Theater, 1931, P.O. Lewis, 961 Broxton Avenue, Westwood Village.

Wardman Theater, 1932, David Bushnell, 7038 Greenleaf Avenue, Whittier.

Fox Theater, 1931, Balch & Stanberry, southwest corner of Garey and Third streets, Pomona.

Alex Theater, 1924-25, by Arthur G. Lindley & Chas. R. Selkirk, Streamline front added in 1939, 268 N. Brand Boulevard, Glendale.

Art Deco Community Buildings and Structures

Sixth Street Viaduct Bridge, 1932, engineers Louis Blume and Merrill Butler, Sixth Street between Alameda and Soto streets.

Los Angeles Public Library (now the Richard J. Riordan Central Library), 1922-26, Bertram G. Goodhue and Carleton M. Winslow, located at the southeast corner of S. Flower and W. Fifth streets.

The Elks Building (now Park Plaza Hotel), 1923-24, Curlett and Beelman, 607 Park View Street, Los Angeles.

Canoga Park Post Office, 1938, Louis A. Simon, supervising architect, located at the northwest corner of Sherman Way and Jordan Avenue; includes the WPA mural *Palomino Ponies* by Maynard Dixon, 1942.

Valley Municipal Building, 1932, Peter K. Schabarum, 14410 Sylvan Street, Van Nuys.

Gates Chemistry Laboratory (now Administration Building), 1917, and the Gates Annex, 1927, by Goodhue Associates, located at the California Institute of Technology, Pasadena.

The Bridges Auditorium, 1931, by William Templeton Johnson, Pomona College, Claremont.

Green Dog & Cat Hospital, circa 1936, 1514 W. Slauson Avenue, Los Angeles.

Saint Mary's Hospital, 1935-37, J.E. Loveless, located at the north end of Linden Street at Nineteenth Street, Long Beach.

Detail of façade and neon sign, Pantages Theatre, 1929, designed by B. Marcus Priteca. *Elizabeth McMillian*

The ticket booth and ornate terrazzo paving of the El Rey Theatre. *Elizabeth McMillian*

The El Rey Theatre, exterior. *Elizabeth McMillian*

Art Deco Religious Buildings

B'Nai David Synagogue and School Building, circa 1929, south side of Pico Boulevard at Swall Street, Baldwin Hills.

Westwood Hills Congregational Church, 1928, northwest corner of Westwood Boulevard and LaGrange Avenue, Westwood.

Our Lady of Lourdes Roman Catholic Church, 1930, Lester R. Scherer, 3773 Third Street, Boyle Heights.

North Glendale Methodist Church, 1941, Harry W. Pierce, northwest corner of Glenoaks Street and Central Avenue, Glendale.

Church of the Brethren, 1930, Robert Orr, Strange and Inslee, southwest corner of Fifth and E streets, LaVerne.

Art Deco Monuments

Wrigley Monument, 1924, Avalon Canyon Road, Santa Catalina Island.

New Calvary Cemetery & Mausoleum, 1927, Ross Montgomery, 4201 E. Whittier Boulevard, Boyle Heights.

Home of Peace Cemetery, 1931, 4334 Whittier Boulevard, Whittier.

Tujunga American Legion Hall, circa 1928, 10039 Pinewood Avenue, Tujunga.

Inglewood Memorial Park, 1933-40, structures on north side by Walter E. Eekes, northeast corner of Manchester and Prairie avenues.

Fountain, 1930, Jock Peters, south side of Blackbird Way, south of Meadowlark, Calabasas.

Art Deco Apartments

Sunset Tower Apartment Building (now the Argyle Hotel), 1929-31, Leland A. Bryant, 18358 Sunset Blvd. at Kings Road, West Hollywood.

Montecito Apartment Building, 1931, Marcus Miller, 6650 Franklin Avenue, Hollywood.

Los Feliz Manor Apartment Building, 1929, Jack Grundfor, 4643 Los Feliz Boulevard, Los Feliz.

Apartment Building, circa 1928, 1650 Echo Park Avenue, Echo Park.

Apartment Building, circa 1928, northwest corner of Third Street and Mansfield Avenue, Los Angeles.

Apartment Building, 1930, J. Clarence Smale, 364 S. Cloverdale Avenue, Los Angeles.

Apartment Building., circa 1928, southeast corner of Rossmore and Rosewood streets, Los Angeles.

The Ravenswood, circa 1928, 570 Rossmore Avenue, Los Angeles.

Val d'Amour Apartment Building, 1928, by G.W. Powers, 854 S. Oxford Avenue, Los Angeles.

Marlinex Apartment Building, circa 1930, 938 S. Lake Street, Los Angeles.

Apartment Building, circa 1925, on N. Soto Street, north of Folsom Street, Los Angeles.

The Sunset Tower (now the Argyle Hotel), 1929-31, designed by Leland A. Bryant. *Elizabeth McMillian*

Exterior detail of the Sunset Tower. *Elizabeth McMillian*

Exterior detail of the 1929-31 Sunset Tower. *Elizabeth McMillian*

Exterior detail of the Sunset Tower. *Elizabeth McMillian*

The porte cochere was added to the original Sunset Tower (now the Argyle Hotel). *Elizabeth McMillian*

A new gate copies the chevron pattern of the windows of the Sunset Tower. *Elizabeth McMillian*

Los Feliz Manor Apartment Building, 1929, designed by Jack Gundfor. *Elizabeth McMillian*

Entrance detail of the Echo Park Apartments. *Elizabeth McMillian*

Echo Park Apartments, circa 1928. *Elizabeth McMillian*

The Ravenswood Apartments, circa 1928, once the residence of, and owned by, Mae West. *Elizabeth McMillian*

Detail of the façade of the Ravenswood Apartments. *Elizabeth McMillian*

Mansfield Avenue Apartments, circa 1928. *Elizabeth McMillian*

Art Deco Houses

Smith House, 1929-30, J. Clarence Smale, northwest corner of Second Street and Hudson Avenue, Hancock Park.

House, circa 1927, located at 2414 E. Glenoaks Boulevard at Sleepy Hollow Terrace, Glendale.

The Smith House, 1929-30, designed by J. Clarence Smale. *Elizabeth McMillian*

Parking entrance to the Smith House. *Elizabeth McMillian*

Side view of the Smith House with decorative window to entrance porch. *Elizabeth McMillian*

Streamline Style

Streamline Exposition and Sports Buildings

An exposition-style meeting hall is Los Angeles' key example of the Streamline Style, the Pan-Pacific Auditorium, 1935-38, designed by Walter Wurdeman and Weldon Becket and located at 7600 Beverly Boulevard. It was a large box-like auditorium with four fin-shaped pylons or towers on its entrance façade. This Streamline style derived from similar designs at the Chicago World's Fair of 1933. After serving as a public hall until 1972 when the downtown Convention Center was built, the Pan-Pacific was almost completely destroyed by fire in May 1989. It had been named to the National Register of Historic Places and was slated for a $22-million face-lift when the fire occurred. The Pan-Pacific was partially restored by local architect Jeffrey Kalban as a recreation center, which opened in Spring 2002. Now an iconic image of the Streamline Style, the replicated structure restores the four-pylon-entrance façade now integrated into a new recreation center.

Before the Streamline Style evolved in Los Angeles, the Memorial Coliseum in Exposition Park was designed by John & Donald B. Parkinson in 1921-23 as a simplified Classical structure that lost its decorative detail purely by the architects' no-frills, straightforward approach to the building type. The structure was further developed in order to entice – and then provide extra seating for – the Olympic Games, held in Los Angeles in 1932. Its early Streamline leanings and massive curving form earn it a place in the Streamline Style.

Other Streamline Moderne sports-exposition-type buildings include the Pasadena Winter Garden (now a storage facility), 1940, by Cyril Bennett and located on the Arroyo Parkway at Cordova Street; the clubhouse and grandstand of the 1937 Hollywood Turf Club in Inglewood, designed by Stiles O. Clements with additions by Fred Barlow, Jr., and landscape by Edward Huntsman-Trout; as well as the Los Angeles County Fairgrounds, located in Pomona. While much modified, most of the mid-1930s buildings have Streamline elements as does the sculpture near Gate 3 of the fairgrounds, which is a 1939 work by Lawrence Tenney Stevens.

The original Pan-Pacific Auditorium, 1935-38, designed by Walter Wurdeman and Weldon Becket. *Tom Zimmerman Collection*

An aerial view of the simplified Classical Los Angeles Coliseum, designed in 1921-23 by John & Donald B. Parkinson, renovated in 1931-32 to appear Streamline and entice the Olympic Games. *Tom Zimmerman Collection*

The entrance gates to the Los Angeles Coliseum. *California State Library*

Streamline Transport Structures and Gas Stations

One of the finest Moderne buildings to merge the regional Spanish style with the emerging Streamline Style was the Union Passenger Terminal, east of downtown Los Angeles on Alameda Street. It was designed and built between 1934 and 1939 by John & Donald B. Parkinson with J.H. Christie, H.L. Gilman and R.J. Wirth. Artist Herman Sachs was the color consultant and Tommy Tomson did the original landscape architecture. The massive mission-like form of the building is enhanced by a 135-foot clock and observation tower. The arches, courtyards, decorative tiles and built-in furnishings are all designed in a Streamline Moderne fashion.

During the Streamline era, gas stations were rendered as factory-produced industrial products with efficient-looking steel frames, aluminum and porcelain panels, cantilevered canopies, and boxlike service and sales areas. Graphic signs were attenuated along the canopies or projected from the roof, sometimes as towers, to be seen from several blocks away. The late 1930s gas stations were Machine Age products that indulged in commercial appeal for the fast-moving automotive customer and were frequently accompanied by motels and cafes. Unfortunately, few Streamline stations remain, as change of ownership and advertising styles produce frequent remodelings. The remnants of Streamline styling are visible in the West Hollywood gas station, circa 1935, at 8176 Melrose Avenue, and the Alhambra gas station, circa 1938, at the northwest corner of Valley Boulevard and Garfield.

An imported English Art Deco-Streamline Moderne structure much worth comparing to local Streamline structures is the ocean liner the *Queen Mary*, 1934, located at 1126 Queen's Way Drive, Pier J, in the Long Beach Harbor.

A corridor leading to the tracks of the Union Passenger Terminal, 1934-39. *Tom Zimmerman*

Los Angeles' Union Passenger Terminal, 1934-39, designed by John & Donald B. Parkinson with J.H. Christie, H.L. Gilman, and R.J. Wirth. *Elizabeth McMillian*

Pylon lights with Streamline graphics at Los Angeles' Union Passenger Terminal. *Elizabeth McMillian*

An interior view of Los Angeles' Union Passenger Terminal. *Elizabeth McMillian*

One of the towers that originally decorated the 1930s Sixth Street Bridge. *California State Library*

A detail of the Sixth Street Bridge as it exists today. *Tom Zimmerman*

Streamline Supermarkets, Restaurants, and Department Stores

Planning for a motorized public was the dominant aim of designers of markets, supermarkets, restaurants, and department stores and shops. The Streamline Moderne was an appropriate style with its horizontality, curved corners, large glazed walls, and glass bricks. It worked well for a new category of drive-in architecture.

While Frank Lloyd Wright's Yucca-Vine Market of 1928 was one of the earliest to orient shopping to the car, Stiles O. Clements tackled the new architectural form of the supermarket, making his car-friendly, auto-oriented design a set formula for others to follow. For Ralphs Supermarkets, he designed buildings as horizontal boxes that opened to the street and to the parking lot by continuous walls of plate-glass windows and glass doors, and welcomed traffic from the parking lot with canopy entrances. On one corner would be a vertical sign treated as a large tower. Thin horizontal bands of planes and lines produced some sense of ornament and modernity. Clements' Carl's Supermarket Building on W. Sixth Street in MacArthur Park was an early example of his work. Built in 1933, its image merged both Art Deco Moderne and Streamline elements. Also, the 1940 supermarket building on the northeast corner of Pico and La Cienega boulevards, attributed to Clements, is a Streamline work with fin-like signage and relief sculpture that is modeled on a Hugh Ferris skyscraper from his 1929 book, *Metropolis of Tomorrow.*

A few 1920s restaurants acknowledged the parking lot and the automobile, but in the Streamline 1930s, a number were planned so that customers could eat in their cars, reducing the design to a dominant vertical sign, an enclosed boxlike service/sales area, and a cantilevered canopy (or multiples of these) for servicing the car and driver. By the late '30s and early '40s, drive-ins were built on many of Los Angeles' favorite automotive strips, such as Christy's (demolished) at the corner of Crenshaw Boulevard and Western Avenue. The circular 1937 Carpenter's on Sunset Boulevard (demolished) was one of the best examples of the unique building type as well as the Streamline Moderne Style. As well, the 1938 Carl's Sea Air Café (demolished) in Santa Monica offered a motel and gas station along with its Pacific Coast Highway Streamline diner and counter service.

In department store design, the May Company, 1940 (located on the northeast corner of Wilshire Boulevard and Farifax Avenue), took advantage of the power of advertising learned from supermarket signs. At the major corner, the architect, Albert C. Martin, created a golden tower that was based on a '30s perfume bottle. With its sign, particularly lit at night, the corner element dominated the structure. The neutral box behind it, sheathed in travertine with large glazed windows and bands of projecting metal framing, served as a Streamline backdrop for the corner tower.

Embracing the automobile and providing it with three levels of parking, the 1938 Streamline Sears Roebuck store (now demolished) on Pico Boulevard was designed by John S. Redden and John G. Raben. The ideal suburban department store as a box-like structure in a subdued Streamline Style became a backdrop for the automobile which could be parked in the large parking lot on the west side or on the roof of the store.

Opposite page, top:
Before: The early twentieth century Robinson's Department Store. *California State Library*

Opposite page, bottom:
After: The reserved Streamlined renovation of the Robinson's Department Store, early 1930s. *California State Library*

Before: The early twentieth century Mullen & Bluett Store. *California State Library*

Other Streamline Stores and Shops

Chandler's Shoe Store, circa 1938, Marcus P. Miller, northwest corner of Wilshire Boulevard and Cloverdale Avenue.

Royal Laundry Bldg, 1927, with additions from circa 1935, Gordon B. Kaufmann, 443 S. Raymond, Pasadena.

Bryan's Cleaners, 1938, Eliot Construction Co., 544 Arroyo Pkwy, Pasadena.

Rexall Drug Company Building, 1935, B.D. Bixby, 6800-04 Hollywood Boulevard at Highland Avenue.

Owl Drug Company Building, 1934, Morgan, Walls & Clements, 6380-84 Hollywood Boulevard at Cahuenga.

Automobile Showroom Building (originally for Volkswagen), circa 1937, northwest corner of Maple Drive and Olympic Boulevard, Beverly Hills.

Store Building, circa 1937, mid-block on the north side of Rose Avenue between Fourth and Fifth streets, Venice.

Store Building, circa 1937, 1332-80 Main Street, between San Juan and Horizon avenues, Venice.

Opposite page, bottom:
After: The early 1930s Streamline renovation of the first floor storefront of the Mullen & Bluett Store. *California State Library*

MULLEN & BLUETT
TAILOR

Carl's at the Beach (also called Carl's Sea Air Café), a 1934-35 Streamline drive-in restaurant, formerly located on Pacific Coast Highway in Santa Monica. *Tom Zimmerman Collection*

Carl's drive-in also included a motel and gas station. *Tom Zimmerman Collection*

The counter on the interior of Carl's drive-in. *Tom Zimmerman Collection*

The restaurant of Carl's drive-in, with built-in booths and a cocktail bar. *Tom Zimmerman Collection*

Christy's, a 1930s Streamline drive-in restaurant, formerly located at Crenshaw Boulevard and Western Avenue. *Tom Zimmerman Collection*

The May Company, 1940, designed by Albert C. Martin. *Elizabeth McMillian*

The Fred Harvey restaurant at Los Angeles' Union Passenger Terminal, 1934-39, designed by John & Donald B. Parkinson with J.H. Christie, H.L. Gilman, and R.J. Wirth. *Tom Zimmerman*

Booths at the Fred Harvey restaurant at Los Angeles' Union Passenger Terminal, 1934-39. *Tom Zimmerman*

Streamline Theatres

While Los Angeles' first drive-in theatre opened in 1934 at the corner of Pico and Westwood, the enclosed auditorium remained the most popular form through the Streamline era and theatre designer S. Charles Lee received a majority of its commissions. His 1931 Florence theatre (now demolished) was oriented to both the street and the automobile by providing a motor driveway leading to an enclosed forecourt, and then to parking at the rear of the building. Lee repeated this auto-orientation a number of times during the 1930s, as at his 1939 Academy Theatre in Inglewood at 3100 Manchester Boulevard. Though much remodeled, it is still Streamline and the 125-foot-high tower remains the same. The tower is made of stucco-sheathed cylinders encircling one another and originally was lit by blue neon tubes. To garner auto attention, in Westwood's 1930s Bruin Theater, Lee made use of the semicircular façade and the lighted marquee, and in Sherman Oaks' 1939 La Reina Theater, he employed the multi-sided marquee supporting a crown.

Other Streamline architects of note also employed Lee's auto-orientation to theatre design. Paul Lazlo's 1939 Crenshaw Theatre extended the marquee to the side, where customers could be let off and picked up under the canopy, and Gordon B. Kaufmann designed the 1937 Earl Carroll Theatre in Hollywood to face the side parking lot. Clarence J. Smale continued Lee's exaggerated form of the marquee and signage at his Loyola Theater, 1946, in which the marquee and its curved sign are the building. (The building has now been remodeled, but the marquee remains.) Balch and Stanberry also used Lee's emphasis on the tower and dramatic lighting for the Boulevard Theater, circa 1937, which is an angular interpretation of the Streamline Style.

The 1939 Academy Theatre in Inglewood, designed by S. Charles Lee, as it appeared in the 1960s. *California State Library*

Streamline Programmatic Buildings

During the 1920s, Los Angeles saw the production of small-scale buildings that were symbolic of their products and could be seen by the customer speeding by in an automobile. These programmatic buildings ranged from chili bowls for Mexican restaurants to igloos for selling ice cream. With the Streamline Style's interest in appearing like factory-made products or having the dynamism of ships, cars, trains, and planes, it would be expected that some architects and designers would take the style literally.

One small programmatic piece is a small Streamline shop on Wilshire Boulevard, The Dark Room, 1938, by Marcus P. Miller, which is crisply designed to appear like an industrially-designed product. The store façade appears like a camera with curved corners, shiny black vitrolite surface, and a central lens (circular window) outlined in silver trim.

Architect Robert V. Derrah designed two delightful large-scale programmatic works which are both listed as Los Angeles Historic-Cultural Heritage monuments. His Crossroads of the World, 1936, at 6671 Sunset Boulevard in Hollywood is a complex of shops based on the theme of a dominant Streamline Moderne ship sailing into the Sunset Strip. Along the ship's sides are shops made to appear like a quaint village of two-story Spanish Colonial, Tudor, and French Provincial houses with a lighthouse. On its prow, the Streamline ship features a tall open tower (like those used on the Streamline movie theatres). This tower supports a lighted globe. Derrah showed great innovation in his approach to a pedestrian mall and great understanding of the advertising effect of a building's structure.

Derrah's Coca-Cola Bottling Company Plant, 1936-37, is the ultimate Streamline decorated box, using the ship allusion literally. Located on Central Avenue, the plant is actually made up of several old buildings that were added onto and remodeled. The ocean liner imagery includes a ship's bridge, metal railings, portholes, metal ship doors, and the suggestion of rivets. The undecorated, efficient nautical form was appropriate for the production of Coke bottles via machines and conveyor-belts, and turned out to be a good public relations and advertising tool.

Good Streamline product design was a goal of 1930s designers and Marcus P. Miller turned the high-tech look of the black and silver camera into a building for The Dark Room, 1938, located on Wilshire Boulevard. *Elizabeth McMillian*

CROSSROADS
6671 OF THE WORLD 6671
UNIQUE
OFFICES
(323) 463-5611

Opposite page:
Crossroads of the World, Robert V. Derrah's 1938 project, features a ship – with a tall tower – arriving onto Hollywood's Sunset Boulevard. *Elizabeth McMillian*

A side view of the Crossroads of the World shows the deck-like sides of the central building which face out to two-story shops of various European designs. *Elizabeth McMillian*

The programmatic Streamline work of architect Robert V. Derrah is represented by his ship-like Coca-Cola Bottling Company Plant, located on Central Avenue near downtown Los Angeles. *Elizabeth McMillian*

A detail view of the side of the 1936-37 Coca-Cola Bottling Company Plant. *Elizabeth McMillian*

Streamline Office Buildings

No other region of the country was as open to the new Streamline images as Los Angeles. The city's economy improved by the late 1930s and new buildings as well as renovated ones reflected the desire to build anew with the progressive style. No single architect dominated the scene; instead, a number of men utilized this style:

Robert V. Derrah built the non-programmatic, highly restrained Southern Counties Gas Company Building, 1939-40, on Flower Street. (It has since been heavily altered.)

The Swiss émigré-New York architect William Lescaze was brought in to design the CBS Building, 1937-38. It was a blend of the Modern International Style and the Moderne with its cubic form, smooth surfaces, ribbon windows, and its Streamline Style-dominant projecting CBS sign.

John C. Austin's 1938-39 NBC Building (now demolished) contrasted the International Style steel-and-glass elements of the nearby CBS Building. It was very Streamline in its white stucco volumes, rounded walls, and graphics.

Stiles Clements designed the 1936 Radio Station Building located at 133-41 N. Vermont Avenue. It was one of Los Angeles' more expressive examples of the style with a central pylon tower.

Gordon B. Kaufmann was the architect of the Aluminum Company of America Building, 1938, in Vernon, built with cast aluminum elements. He was also responsible for the utilitarian Vultee Aircraft Plant building, which had interiors and a mural by Kem Weber.

A vintage postcard shows bold signage incorporated into the design of the CBS that gives a Streamline edge to the otherwise International Style appearance of the building. It was designed by William Lescaze with George Howe and built 1937-38. *Tom Zimmerman Collection*

Another 1930s postcard reveals the Streamline curves, banding and glass-block that characterized the NBC Building, 1938-39, designed by John C. Austin. *Tom Zimmerman Collection*

A view of the NBC Building (now demolished). *Tom Zimmerman Collection*

Some of the most imaginative Streamline commercial structures include:

The Lane-Wells Company Building, 1938-39, by William E. Myer, in Huntington Park, had a strong horizontal emphasis that was contrasted with tall pylons at the entrances. The reinforced concrete building had rounded corners and large glass areas. The architect provided a park-like setting to remove the stigma of the old-fashioned factory.

The Merle Norman Building, 1935-36, designed by George Parr, on Main Street in Venice, was a remodeling of an existing brick building. Ocean liners inspired the design and the south corner of the building appears like a ship with a round tower over an open bridge.

The Eagles Building, located on the northwest corner of Catalina Avenue and Garnet Street in Redondo Beach, was a pure example of the Streamline Moderne, although it was built in 1949. All the windows were connected by horizontal bands and the entrances contrasted the horizontality with emphatic vertical projections which rose up over the parapets.

The 1947 Gerry Building by Maurice Fleischman, located at 910 Los Angeles Street, was another late example. A majority of the façade is glazed with curved corners.

A late example of the Streamline Style that echoed the work of Erich Mendelsohn was the Gerry Building, 1947, designed by Maurice Fleischman. *Tom Zimmerman*

Erich Mendelsohn's Herpich Store Building, Berlin, 1924, shows the banded front and curved-glass sides similar to the 1947 Gerry Building in LA. *Sheldon Cheney, The New World Architecture, 1930*

Other Streamline Office Buildings, Public Buildings, and Schools

The Radio Building, circa 1941, north side of the 4500 block Pico Boulevard, Los Angeles.

Owens-Illinois Pacific Building, 1937, H.H. Brunnier, northeast corner of E. Fruitland Avenue and S. Soto Street, Vernon.

Aeroscopic Building, circa 1935, 5245 W. San Fernando Road, Glendale.

Carnation Research Building, 1952-53, 8015 Van Nuys Boulevard at Lorne Street, Los Angeles.

Telesound Studio, circa 1945, 6926 Melrose Avenue, Los Angeles.

Commercial Building, circa 1935, 9169 Sunset Boulevard, Beverly Hills.

Commercial Building, circa 1938, located at the northwest corner of Pacific Avenue and Sixteenth Street, Santa Monica.

Woodbury College Building, 1937, Claude Beelman, 1027 Wilshire, MacArthur Park.

Swimming Pool Building, Beverly Hills High School, circa 1937, Stiles O. Clements, between Heath Avenue and Moreno Drive above Olympic, Beverly Hills.

Pepperdine College (old campus; several examples of Streamline Moderne), 1937, Thomas Cooper; Katherine Bashford, and Frederick Barlow, Jr., landscape architects, west of Seventy-ninth Street and S. Vermont Avenue, Inglewood.

Municipal Light, Water and Power Building, circa 1937, 313 S. Brand Boulevard, San Fernando.

Department of Water and Power Building, 1939, attributed to S. Charles Lee, 5108 Lankershim Boulevard, San Fernando.

The Merle Norman Building, 1935-36, designed by George Parr. *Elizabeth McMillian*

Streamline Apartments

The 1930s saw an increase in apartments and multiple housing units which thoroughly established Los Angeles' tradition of the wood-framed, stucco-sheathed box. The best ones created indoor-outdoor connections with patios, terraces, balconies, and courtyard, and the worst and most repetitive were soon enhanced by the region's fast-growing vegetation. The city and county also became involved in low-cost housing in 1937 after Congress passed President Roosevelt's Lanham Act creating the United States Housing Authority. Between 1938 and late 1941, Los Angeles built twelve public housing projects, such as The Ramona Gardens, 1938-40, and Aliso Village, 1941-42, which brought together a talented group of designers including Lloyd Wright. Among both private projects and public housing, corner windows, horizontal balconies, and simple details suggest the late 1930s Streamline Moderne Style.

Among the private projects, some designers worked exclusively in the Streamline Moderne Style. Milton J. Black was perhaps the best designer in this mode. The most exquisite of his apartment houses was the Mauritania, 1936, located at 520-22 Rossmore Avenue, which was named after, and inspired by, the famous ocean liner. Today, it still retains the curved walls, banding, deck-like elements, and graphic signage of the ship, and has been named a Los Angeles Historic-Cultural Heritage Monument.

Although Black's 1936 apartment building at Hobart and Ninth streets once included a row of fins on the main façade, his other apartment buildings are more reserved and typical of the Streamline Style, such as the 1938 project he designed with R. Borman located at 462 S. Cochran Avenue; or Black's U-planned Westwood-Ambassador Apartments (10427 Wilshire Boulevard), completed in 1940; or his various 1930s apartments located at 100 N. Harper Street, 127 S. Kings Road, and 3919 W. Eighth Street – all of which remain in fair to excellent condition today.

Other Streamline Apartments and Hotels

Apartment Building, 1936, 1146-52 S. Westmoreland Avenue, MacArthur Park.

Bungalow Court, circa 1937, 428-32 S. Burlington Avenue, MacArthur Park.

Voss Apartments, 1937-47, 935 Eleventh Street near Washington Avenue, Santa Monica.

Apartment Building, circa 1940, southwest corner of First Street and S. Kings Road, West Hollywood.

Apartment Building, circa 1938, Carl Kay, 1941-43 Mariposa Avenue, Los Angeles.

Apartment Building, circa 1937, Wesley Eager, 4116 Franklin Avenue, Los Angeles.

Apartment Building, 1939, J. Knauer, 423-34 Franklin Avenue, Los Angeles.

Apartment Building, circa 1935, 814 Plymouth Boulevard, Los Angeles.

Apartment Building, circa 1935, 3919 W. Eighth Street, Los Angeles.

Apartment Building, 1936, Earl D. Stonerod, 1554-60 S. St. Andrews Place, Los Angeles.

Garden Apartment Building, circa 1936, 1001-09 Malcolm Avenue, Westwood.

Apartment Building, 1928, 917 First Street, Long Beach.

Shangri-La Apartments (now Hotel), 1937-40, William E. Foster, Ocean Avenue at Arizona Street, Santa Monica.

Baldwin Motel, circa 1934, 12823 Washington Boulevard, Culver City.

Shangri-La Apartments (now Hotel), 1937-40, designed by William E. Foster. *Elizabeth McMillian*

Façade of the Mauritania Apartments, 1936, designed by Milton J. Black. *Elizabeth McMillian*

Corner windows of the Mauritania Apartments. *Elizabeth McMillian*

Entrance is along one side of the three-story Mauritania Apartments. *Elizabeth McMillian*

Stair leading to the upper deck of the Mauritania Apartments. *Elizabeth McMillian*

Landmark plaque of the Mauritania Apartments. *Elizabeth McMillian*

Apartments, 1134 Seventeenth Street, Santa Monica. *Elizabeth McMillian*

Apartment building on Cochran, 1938, designed by Milton J. Black and R. Borman. *Elizabeth McMillian*

A 1930s Kings Road apartment building designed by Milton J. Black. *Elizabeth McMillian*

Streamline Houses

The detached single-family dwelling was the ideal of most Los Angeles residents, and although the number of Modern and Moderne houses built in the area in the 1930s was minimal compared to the number of Spanish, Tudor, and French Provincial designs, there was no other region in the United States that was so open to the new styles and had the architectural talent to draw on for creating it.

It was apparent nationally that the body of 1930s work – both Modern and the Moderne – constituted a rich Los Angeles movement. The domestic architecture varied from the complex spatial organizations of R.M. Schindler, the International Style of Neutra, and the concrete-block experimentation of Lloyd Wright to the modern variations of J.R. Davidson, Paul Laszlo, Raphael Soriano, Gregory Ain, and Harwell H. Harris, to the Streamline Moderne, built by a cadre of lesser-known talents such as Milton Black, Jock Peters, Wesley Eager, Edgar Bissantz, Adrian Wilson, Carl Kay, J. Knauer, Robert Derrah, and others.

The dividing line between the Modern and the Moderne tended to be very fuzzy. Many of the renowned residential architects – some of whom also produced period styles – adopted images of the Moderne. The curved walls, corner windows, glass bricks, pipe rail (or metal railings), and portholes infiltrated even the plainest of contractor-designed stucco-sheathed boxes. Common to all were the free-flowing interior spaces and the sustained relationship between the indoors and outdoors.

H. Roy Kelley was an architect who was known for his period revival work and yet he designed the 1934 Phillips House in San Marino to be Streamline Moderne Style in image, scale, and detailing. This rare exception to his norm was joined by the 1935 Model House he designed with Edgar F. Bissantz and H.G. Spielman. The house was erected for the first housing exhibition held at the Pan-Pacific Auditorium. After the house was won in a raffle, it was moved to a hillside site in the San Fernando Valley. It typified many 1930s Los Angeles houses which were essentially California Ranch houses brought up to date by including elements such as portholes and glass-brick associated with the Streamline Moderne.

One Moderne classic was the Maharajah of Indore's 1939 house located near Los Angeles in Santa Ana. Earlier, in India, the Maharajah had become interested in the Moderne Style and had the interiors of his palace, located some 350 miles northeast of Bombay, redesigned by DiStijl architect Eckhart Muthesius. The Maharajah amassed an enormous collection of Modern and Moderne furnishings by the Dutch architect, as well as by Le Corbusier, Emile-Jacques Ruhlmann, Eileen Gray, Louis Sognot, and others. When the young Indian ruler visited Los Angeles in the late 1930s, he became enamored with the modern feel of the region and had architect Donald Beach Kirby build him a Moderne house in Santa Ana. Unfortunately, the house, which has since been remodeled, did little to further mainstream acceptance of the Streamline Style for residential design.

Modern and Modernist architects created houses that fit into the parameters of Streamline Moderne design. (Also see the section "The Fine Line Between Modern and Moderne," above.) Among these architects were:

• Lloyd Wright, who brought Moderne design elements to a number of his works, for instance, the 1935 Colbert House at 615 N. Faring Road, and the 1940 Greer House, 1940, which included porthole windows. Wright's 1963 Johnson House continued his interest in the ancient Mayan made Moderne, like his Art Deco/Streamline-related 1926 Sowden House and 1926-28 Samuels-Navarro House.

• Douglas Honnold, who imparted an Art Deco-Streamline sensibility to the 1929 Dolores Del Rio - Cedric Gibbons house he designed with Gibbons in the Palisades.

A 1936 Willliam Kesling-designed residence on Harper Avenue takes advantage of the corner site with its curved window, stepped-back volumes and upper terrace. *Elizabeth McMillian*

•Raphael S. Soriano, whose 1935 Lipetz House in Silverlake had a Streamline Moderne ship's bridge and metal railings that perpetuated the nautical theme.

•Harwell Hamilton Harris, who included curved walls, a spiral staircase and metal railing in the 1937 Pacific Palisades house he designed for John Entenza.

•Rodney Walker, whose 1940 Lohrie House in Bel Air was a California Ranch House with Moderne windows and extended horizontal planes.

•Jock Peters, the émigré decorator, whose 1934 Shepard House in San Marino is one of the few Streamline houses he ever built.

• William Kesling. Vernacular acceptance of the Streamline Style created a number of talented contractor-builders, the best and most prolific of whom was the self-trained William Kesling. Of the thirty-five projects that he built, twenty have survived, but not all of these are totally intact and only a few retain their original plans and fixtures. Among the number of Kesling's houses that have been preserved and renovated to retain their original character are his 1936 duplex located at 754-56 Harper Avenue; the Ulm House, 1937, at 3606 Amesbury Road; and the group of three houses, 1935-38, in the Silverlake district in the 1500 block of Easterly Terrace. Kesling's 1935 Johnstone House, located at 3311 Lowry Road, was tastefully renovated by its owner, Patrick Pascal, who recently wrote *William Kesling's Modern Structures, Popularizing Modern Design in Southern California, 1934-1962*. The book has done much to fuel the contemporary interest in early Modernism and raise the reputation of William Kesling and his works.

Other Streamline Houses

Cernitz House, 1938, Milton J. Black, 60 Amalfi Drive, Pacific Palisades.

Two Houses, circa 1937, Carl Kay, High Tower Road, flanking the High Tower, central Hollywood.

House, 1937-39, Barcume and King, 7777 Firenze Avenue, Hollywood Hills.

House, circa 1938, 5740 Whitlock Avenue, Los Angeles.

House, circa 1937, 936 E. Ocean Boulevard, Long Beach.

House, circa 1936, 376 Orlena Avenue, Long Beach.

House, 1935, Kenneth Worthen, Sr., 4217 Navajo Street, Toluca Lake.

Bungalow, circa 1935, northwest corner of Moorpark Stret and Vista del Monte Avenue, Sherman Oaks.

House, circa 1937, southeast corner of Second Street and Linda Vista, Alhambra.

Two Bungalows, 1935, 246 & 248 Jesse Avenue at Victory, Glendale.

The living room of architect Tom Michali's Streamline Duplex apartment, designed in 1938 by Harold Joysmith. *Elizabeth McMillian*

On one side of the living room of the Tom and Nancy Michali residence is a staircase with a curved chrome stair rail. *Elizabeth McMillian*

The dining room is raised one step from the living room level. *Elizabeth McMillian*

Windows wrap around a corner of the Michali dining room. *Elizabeth McMillian*

A decorative floral sconce in the dining room is one Art Deco remnant in the Streamline style Michali apartment. *Elizabeth McMillian*

A view into the remodeled kitchen shows the original curved wall. *Elizabeth McMillian*

A swinging door and built-in shelving are a part of the original kitchen, while the new cabinetry and slender counter suit the streamline design. *Elizabeth McMillian*

The pastel bath of the Michali Duplex features built-in cabinets. *Elizabeth McMillian*

A step leads up to the bathtub making it appear sunken. The riser tiles are ribbed. *Elizabeth McMillian*

Tube lights flank the typical 1930s mirrored medicine cabinet. *Elizabeth McMillian*

A terrace with metal railing is located off the master bedroom of the Michali Duplex. *Elizabeth McMillian*

Opposite page:
The Johnstone Residence, 1935, designed by William Kesling. *Elizabeth McMillian*

Glass corner windows, banded volumes, and projecting canopies are features of Kesling's Streamline Johnstone Residence, now owned by Peter and Julie Pascal. *Elizabeth McMillian*

The Johnstone House entrance hall displays a sliding panel front door and patterned flooring. *Elizabeth McMillian*

A view into the living room of the Johnstone Residence. *Elizabeth McMillian*

SPRINGS MODERN
CRAIG
Modernism Rediscovered

Opposite page:
The living room fireplace of the Johnstone Residence with built-in mantle and shelving and metal banding. *Elizabeth McMillian*

A library niche in one corner of the Johnstone Residence living room. *Elizabeth McMillian*

Broad windows also open one wall of the dining room to the rear terrace. *Elizabeth McMillian*

A window wall opens the living room to the rear terrace and garden. *Elizabeth McMillian*

The Ulm House, 1937, designed by William Kesling, is highlighted by a Streamline semicircular, glass-block stair tower. *Elizabeth McMillian*

The rear façade of the Ulm House. *Elizabeth McMillian*

Angles, built-in shelving, and recessed lighting characterize the Ulm House living room. *Elizabeth McMillian*

A corner of the Ulm House living room shows a wall of windows opening to a raised terrace. The painting is by the resident, artist Beatrice Findlay who, with her husband, Chap Findlay, has restored much of the house to its original condition. *Elizabeth McMillian*

Beatrice Findlay's paintings are also visible in the angled fireplace niche of the Ulm House. *Elizabeth McMillian*

The Ulm House dining room is enclosed on one side by an angled wall. *Elizabeth McMillian*

Corner windows open the dining room to the terrace. *Elizabeth McMillian*

The dining room seen from the outside terrace. *Elizabeth McMillian*

The Ulm House outdoor terrace with pipe-railing. The terrace covering was added later. *Elizabeth McMillian*

The 1936 Ship of the Desert house (Davidson House) in Palm Springs was designed by Los Angeles architects Adrian Wilson and Erle Webster, and was restored by Leo Marmol and Ron Radziner. *Jason Schmidt*

The living room of the 1936 Ship of the Desert house, Palm Springs. *Jason Schmidt*

Furnishings in 1930s style before the fireplace in the living room. *Jason Schmidt*

A bedroom with recessed ceiling light in the Ship of the Desert house. *Jason Schmidt*

The kitchen features a built-in banquette with table. *Jason Schmidt*

The entrance hall of the Ship of the Desert house features a curved rail following the curved wall of the stair. *Jason Schmidt*

PWA and Classical Moderne

The Moderne label also encompasses the numerous PWA and Classical-style buildings built during the last years of the presidency of Herbert Hoover and throughout the Depression years of the '30s, when architects merged the Beaux Arts Classical with the Art Deco and Streamline Moderne. PWA and Classical Moderne styles are closely associated with federal governmental architecture, but they were also employed on private commercial buildings.

These buildings were formal and fundamentally Classical with enough Moderne details to convey a contemporary feeling. Their characteristics include balanced and symmetrical form and classical horizontal proportions. Rather than columns, they used piers, which were occasionally fluted, but usually had no capitals or bases. Surfaces were smooth and often sheathed in sturdy materials like stone, polished marble, granite and terrazzo with terra-cotta detail. Ornament was frequently a program of traditional-style relief sculpture. Windows were rhythmically arranged as vertical, recessed panels and, on the interiors, rich materials, relief work and murals adorned the lobbies and major spaces.

Los Angeles acquired a wealth of these buildings during the '30s, stimulated by the federal government's Works Administration (PWA), which built schools, libraries, and post offices in order to put people back to work. It also benefited from PWA's companion organization, the Works Progress Administration (WPA), which had an Arts Project that resulted in many of the murals and sculptures that began to appear in public squares, lobbies of public buildings, post offices, schools, and libraries.

With this stimulus, Los Angeles retained its optimism through the '30s and became the city of the middle-class dream, well-expressed via the Moderne taste in design.

PWA and Classical Moderne Public Buildings, Utilities, Services, and Monuments

The 1930s renaissance of Los Angeles public architecture resulted from the federal funds parceled out through the PWA or Post Office Department. It encouraged county and city governments to engage in a large-scale building program. Between 1933 and 1939, the PWA provided the state with 221 government buildings – a great number of them built in Southern California – and the style became more monumental, using Greek and Roman sources of architecture rather than the Gothic, which enjoyed some popularity for the soaring character of the Art Deco style.

Torrance City Hall and Municipal Auditorium (now Home Savings Branch Bank), 1936-37, Walker & Eisen, north corner of Cravens and Prado avenues.

Burbank City Hall, 1940-41, William Allen and George Lutzi, southwest corner of Olive and Third streets.

Glendale City Hall, 1940-42, Albert E. Hansen, northwest corner of Broadway and Howard streets.

Santa Monica City Hall, 1938-39, Donald B. Parkinson and J.M. Estep, 1685 Main Street; lobby murals by Stanton Macdonald-Wright.

Griffith Park Observatory and Planetarium, 1935, John C. Austin, Frederick M. Ashley; obelisk and bas-reliefs by Archibald Garner, 1934; murals by Hugo Ballin, 1935, Western Canyon Road, Griffith Park.

Federal Building and Post Office (now United States Federal Courthouse), 1938-40, Louis A. Simon, Gilbert Stanley Underwood; sculpture by James L. Hauser, *The Young Lincoln,* and Archibald Garner, *Law*; northeast corner of Spring and Temple streets, Los Angeles.

United States Naval and Marine Corps Armory, 1939-40, Stiles O. Clements, Stadium Way near Lilac Terrace, Los Angeles.

United States Post Office, Osbourne Station, circa 1928, 1767 Highland Avenue, Central Hollywood.

United States Post Office, Hollywood Branch, 1937, Claude Beelman, Allison & Allison, 1615 Wilcox Avenue, Hollywood.

Santa Monica Post Office, 1937, Neil A. Melick and Robert A. Murray, 1248 Fifth Street at Arizona Avenue, Santa Monica.

Post Office and Federal Building, 1931-32, James A. Wetmore, designed by Hugh R. Davis, northeast corner of Long Beach Boulevard and Third Street, Long Beach.

Whittier Post Office, 1935, Louis A. Simon, northwest corner of Washington and Bailey streets, Whittier.

Post Office Building, 1940, Louis A. Simon, Neal A. Melick, 567 W. Lancaster Street, San Pedro.

United States Customs House and Post Office, 1935, mural by Fletcher Martin, northwest corner of Beacon and Ninth streets, San Pedro.

Police and Fire Station of Venice, circa 1930, northeast corner of Venice Boulevard and Pisani Drive.

Distribution Station #28, Department of Water and Power, 1945-46, engineer G.E. Benker, southeast corner of Cotner Street and Missouri Avenue, Westwood.

Torrance Public Library, 1936, Walker & Eisen, corner of Craven and Post avenues, Torrance.

MacArthur Park Sculpture: *Prometheus*, 1935, Nina Saemundsson, southwest corner of Wilshire Boulevard and Alvarado Street, MacArthur Park.

Municipal Ferry Building (City Hall/Harbor Department Building), 1939-41, east end of Sixth Street at Harbor Boulevard, San Pedro.

Long Beach Airport Terminal, 1940-41, Kenneth S. Wing and W. Horace Austin, (original murals and mosaics by Grace Clements are painted over), west end of Douglas off Lakewood Boulevard, Long Beach.

Sepulveda Control Dam, Water Channels and Control Tower, 1939-41, by United States District Engineer, War Department, just off Burbank Boulevard, north of Sepulveda, to the spillway and tower, Los Angeles.

Los Angeles/University of Southern California Medical Center, 1928-33 and later; Allied Architects: Edwin Bergstrom, Myron Hunt, Pierpont Davis, Sumner P. Hunt, William Richards; 1200 State Street, Lincoln Heights.

St. Luke's Hospital, 1934, Gene Verge, Sr., 2632 E. Washington near Altadena Drive, Pasadena.

The Santa Monica City Hall, 1938-39, designed by John & Donald B. Parkinson and J.M. Estep, is a symmetrical, reserved design enlivened with colorful tile details. *Elizabeth McMillian*

An aerial postcard view of the streamlined and Classical 1935 Griffith Park Observatory and Planetarium designed by John C. Austin and F.M. Ashley. *Tom Zimmerman Collection*

A late 1940s postcard shows the Griffith Observatory capping one of the Hollywood Hills. *Tom Zimmerman Collection*

PWA and Classical Moderne Schools

The greatest number of the PWA Classical structures were public school buildings. Between 1933 and 1939, the PWA provided the state with 140 schools, a great number of which were built in the Los Angeles area. The styles of these were original and innovative, and ranged from the Streamline Moderne of the Thomas Jefferson High School in Los Angeles (O.W. Morgan, J.A. Walls, and Stiles O. Clements, 1936) to the vaguely pre-Columbian Moderne Mark Keppel High School in Alhambra (Keith Marston and Edgar Maybury, 1939).

Roosevelt School, 1935, Marsh, Smith & Powell, 801 Montana Avenue and Lincoln Boulevard, Santa Monica.

El Segundo Elementary School, 1936, northwest corner of Mariposa Avenue and Richmond Street, El Segundo.

Grover Cleveland Elementary School, 1934, Robert H. Ainsworth, 524 Palisade Street, Pasadena

Pier Avenue School, 1939, Marsh, Smith & Powell, southwest corner of Pier Avenue and Pacific Coast Highway, Hermosa Beach.

Robert Louis Stevenson School, circa 1936, west side of Lime Avenue between Fifth and Sixth streets, Long Beach.

Hollywood High School Science Building, 1934-35, Marsh, Smith & Powell; bas-relief by Bartolo Mako; mural *Education*, 1934, by Haldine Douglas; northwest corner of Sunset Boulevard and Highland Avenue, Central Hollywood.

Industrial Arts Building, 1934-36, Hugh R. Davies; mural by Ivan Bartlet and Jean Swiggett; located at Long Beach Polytechnic High School, northeast corner of Atlantic Avenue and Fifteenth Street, Long Beach.

Manual Arts High School, 1934-35, John & Donald B. Parkinson, northwest corner of Vermont Avenue and Forty-second Street, Exposition Park, Los Angeles.

Thomas Jefferson High School, 1936, Stiles O. Clements, 319 E. Forty-first Street, Bell.

Bell High School, 1935, Robert F. Train, southeast corner of Bell and Flora streets, Bell.

Abraham Lincoln High School, 1937-38, Albert C. Martin, 3501 N. Broadway, Lincoln Heights.

Whittier Union High School, 1939-40, William H. Harrison, northeast corner of Philadelphia and Whittier streets, Whittier.

Lincoln School, circa 1935, attributed to William H. Harrison, southeast corner of Broadway and Newlin streets, Whittier.

South Pasadena High School, 1937, Marsh, Smith & Powell; murals by Millard Sheets and sculptured panels by Merrell Gage; southwest corner of Fremont Avenue and Lyndon Street, South Pasdena.

Redondo Beach High School, 1931 and later, Allison & Allison, Pacific Coast Highway between Diamond and Vincent streets, Redondo Beach.

Thomas Jefferson High School, 1936, designed by Stiles O. Clements and located in Bell. *Elizabeth McMillian*

San Pedro High School, 1935-37, Gordon Kaufmann, Leland Street between Fifteenth and Seventeenth streets, San Pedro.

Mark Keppel High School, 1939, Marston & Maybury, 501 Hellman Avenue, Alhambra.

Torrance High School, 1923, 1929 and circa 1935; original building by Farrell and Miller; 1936 Federal Art Project mural entitled *Taos Indian Life* by Anna Katharine Skeele; southwest end of El Prado Avenue at Carson Street, Torrance.

Jefferson Junior High School Building, 1936, northeast corner of Euclid Avenue and Seventh Street, Long Beach.

Alan Hancock Foundation and Memorial Museum, University of Southern California, 1940, Cram & Ferguson, C. Raimond Johnson, Samuel E. Lunden; sculpture by Merrell Gage, USC campus, Los Angeles.

PWA and Classical Moderne Religious Buildings

Church of the Incarnation Roman Catholic Church, 1951, northwest corner of Brand and Glenoaks streets, Glendale.

Pasadena Jewish Temple and Center, 1957, 1434 N. Altadena Drive, just above Washington Boulevard, Pasadena.

San Gabriel Union Church and School, 1936, northwest corner of Las Tunas and Pine streets, San Gabriel.

The 1939 Mark Keppel High School in Alhambra was designed by Keith Marston and Edgar Maybury. *Elizabeth McMillian*

A window with an angled canopy at the Mark Keppel High School. *Elizabeth McMillian*

Enameled relief sculpture by Millard Sheets at the entrance of the Mark Keppel High School. *Elizabeth McMillian*

PWA and Classical Moderne Commercial Buildings

With its monumental allusions, the PWA-Classical Moderne Style worked well for some commercial organizations such as the Times-Mirror organization (*Los Angeles Times*), which chose its site to be affiliated with the power structure of the Civic Center, and the Pacific Coast Stock Exchange, which desired to represent financial power and economic stability. It's more unusual to find that companies like Sunkist, Helms Bakery, and MGM Studios opted for the conservative style. Its power-loaded Classical images apparently offered these companies the sense of quality and value mixed with a dose of modernity.

Sunkist Building (demolished), 1935, Albert R. Walker and Percy Eison; murals by Frank Bowers and Arthur Prunier; Los Angeles.

Times-Mirror Building, 1931-35, Gordon B. Kaufmann; rotunda mural *Newspaper* by Hugo Ballin; southwest corner of Spring and First streets, Los Angeles. (The 1948 addition by Rowland H. Crawford on the northwest corner of Spring and Third streets is also a mellow PWA Moderne style; the 1970-73 modern addition to the west is by William L. Pereira and Associates.)

Pacific Coast Stock Exchange, 1929-30, Samuel E. Lunden; John & Donald B. Parkinson, consulting architects; relief sculpture by Salvatore Cartaino Scarpitta; interior relief sculpture by Wilson Studio and murals by Julian Ellsworth Garnsey; 618 Spring Street, Los Angeles.

Helms Bakery Building, 1930, E.L. Bruner, 8800 Venice Boulevard, Culver City.

MGM Studios (Goldwyn Studios) Building, 1938-39, Claude Beelman, corner of Washington Boulevard and Overland Avenue, Culver City.

National Trust and Savings Building, circa 1935, William H. Harrison, northeast corner of Philadelphia and Greenleaf streets, Whittier.

PWA California State Armory, now Armory Gallery, Bennett & Haskell, 1932, 145 N. Raymond Avenue, Pasadena.

Pacific Mutual Building, 1912, 1937 renovation by John & Donald B. Parkinson, 523 W. Sixth Street, Los Angeles.

Los Angeles Branch, Federal Reserve Bank of San Francisco, 1930, John & Donald B. Parkinson; relief sculpture by Edgar Walter; northwest corner of Olive Street and W. Olympic Boulevard, Los Angeles.

The Classical Moderne Federal Reserve Bank of San Francisco, Los Angeles Branch, 1930, designed by John & Donald B. Parkinson with relief sculpture by Edgar Walter. *Tom Zimmerman*

The monumental 1935 Sunkist Building, now demolished, was designed by Albert Walker and Percy Eisen. *Tom Zimmerman Collection*

Another federal arts project, the sculpture and relief panels at Lafayette Park. *Tom Zimmerman*

Regency Moderne

Also called the Hollywood Regency Style, Regency Moderne combined the sleek surfaces of the Streamline Style with nineteenth-century Regency details. The minimal geometric forms of Modernism were juxtaposed with the delicate attenuated elements and vertical proportions of the stylized neoclassical forms of the Regency period. It often ended up being a mere mixture of Eastern Colonial and the Streamline Moderne.

Regency Moderne was sophisticated and refined, so architects like Sumner Spaulding, Douglas Honnold, and George Russell liked it for houses of upper-middle-class clients. These '30s houses were smaller and more intimate in scale than those of the previous decade. Generally, their plans were clear and axial, and openings were wide. Groups of French doors led out from ground-floor rooms to covered porches and outdoor terraces. The auto entrance usually provided the major means of entering the house while the walkway from the house to the street was secondary.

The style worked well for multiple units, garden apartments, and commercial buildings when it was in the hands of architects like Paul Williams, Gordon Kaufmann, and George Vernon Russell. Williams' Georgian Music Corporation of America Building, 1939-40, while not quite Regency Moderne, expresses the same neoclassical interest. Also, Russell's Star's Dressing Room at Twentieth Century Fox Studios, 1936, his William Morris Agency, 1939, and his 1936 remodeling of Ciro's Restaurant on Sunset Boulevard were typical of the style, along with Kaufmann's 1938 Myron Selznick and Company Building, with interiors by Paul T. Frankl. The Regency Moderne was also effective for store fronts. Russell and Honnold's design of a row of six shops on Rodeo Drive, for example, showed individual façades for each and they were treated to appear like they were interiors.

Other Regency Moderne Buildings

I. Magnin and Company Store Building, 1939, Myron Hunt and H.C. Chambers, located on Wilshire Boulevard, Los Angeles.

Saks Fifth Avenue Store, 1937, John & Donald B. Parkinson, interiors by Paul Williams, 9600 Wilshire Boulevard, Beverly Hills.

Max Factor Building, 1931, 1935 remodel by S. Charles Lee, 1659-66 Highland Avenue, Hollywood.

Bullocks Pasadena, 1947, Wurdeman and Becket; Ruth Shillhorn and Carl McElvy, landscape architects; 401 S. Lake Avenue, Pasadena.

Film Exchange, Inc. Building, circa 1928, southeast corner of Santa Monica Boulevard and Cole Avenue, Hollywood.

Apartment House, 1935, northeast corner of Los Feliz Boulevard and Nella Vista Avenue, Los Feliz.

Park La Brea Housing (Metropolitan Life Housing Development), 1941-42; Towers, 1948-49; Leonard Schultze and Son, and E.T. Heitschmidt; Tommy Tomson, landscape architect; bounded by Third Street, Cochran Avenue, Sixth Street and Fairfax Boulevard, Los Angeles.

Pike House, 1952, George Vernon Russell, 6675 Whitley Terrace, Hollywood.

Pendleton House, 1942, John Woolf, 1032 Beverly Drive, Beverly Hills.

As a subdued Regency Moderne structure, the 1939 I. Magnin store on Wilshire Boulevard presents an elegant classical design contained within a rectangular volume. It was designed by Myron Hunt and W.C. Chambers. *Elizabeth McMillian*

Treating the exterior in a decorated manner like an interior – such as the delicate filigreed windows of the Max Factor Building – caused historian/architect John Chase to label many of the Regency Moderne buildings "exterior decoration." Theatre designer S. Charles Lee gave the building its present appearance when he remodeled a simpler 1931 building in 1935. The interiors are just as elaborate and can be seen today since the building is open to the public as a Hollywood museum. *Elizabeth McMillian*

Department of Water & Power Building, 1935, Frederick L. Roehrig, northeast corner of Sunset Boulevard and Via de la Paz, Pacific Palisades.

Department of Water and Power Building, circa 1937, S. Charles Lee, 2417 Daly Street, Lincoln Heights.

Lou Henry Hoover School, 1938, William H. Harrison; relief panel of *A Pageant of Education* by Bartolo Mako; corner of Camilla Street and Alta Avenue, Whittier.

A detail view of the Max Factor Building showing the choice of rich materials and colors for this Regency Moderne style. *Elizabeth McMillian*

The original structures of the Park La Brea Housing (Metropolitan Life Housing Development), 1941-42, designed by Leonard Schultze and Son, and E.T. Heitschmidt. *Elizabeth McMillian*

At Park La Brea, banding and horizontal windows characterize the abbreviated upper story, while attenuated paired columns decorate the front porches and broadly fluted surrounds define the front doors. *Elizabeth McMillian*

Regency Moderne style apartments on Hillhurst Street in the Los Feliz area blend modern design with Regency-style classicism. *Elizabeth McMillian*

Attenuated paired columns and a split pediment with urn define the Regency style entrance of the Hillhurst Street apartments. *Elizabeth McMillian*

The courtyard of the Hillhurst Street apartment building shows other variations of the Regency style entrance porch. *Elizabeth McMillian*

L.A.'s Moderne Legacy

During the late 1940s of World War II recovery and into the early 1950s, Los Angeles saw an evolving middle-class and *nouveau riche* homes build up in the suburbs of Los Angeles' Westside. It also saw some continuation of the Moderne Style, particularly in its PWA/Classical and Regency versions.

One late Streamline example was Albert Frey's Loewy Residence in nearby Palm Springs. Frey was joined in the desert city by the French-born, New York-based industrial designer Raymond Loewy in 1945. Frey designed a house for the designer in which modern materials and dramatic form were quite inspiring to the late Streamline style as well as contemporary Modern architecture.

Also considered Streamline was A. Quincy Jones' Murphy Buick Showroom and Garage, circa 1949, at 9099 Washington Boulevard and the administration building and library of El Camino College, designed in 1951 by Smith, Powell and Morgridge. These buildings display how well postwar architects applied both the lessons of the Modern Movement and the popular Moderne to create functional designs with contemporary images.

The Silverlake area had a few Moderne commercial buildings along Sunset Boulevard, and in 1958, it became home of Conrad's Drive-In at the corner of Glendale Boulevard and Fletcher Drive. The design by Louis Armet and Eldon Davis referred back to the Streamline drive-ins and has been called the People's Moderne of the 1950s, typical of the period when taste shifted to a look that suited the world of Doris Day movies and Elvis Presley records.

Another tongue-in-cheek term, the Cocktail Lounge Moderne, has been used to describe a '50s Moderne work in Westwood, the Los Angeles Temple of the Church of Jesus Christ of Latter-Day Saints. Located at 10741 Santa Monica Boulevard and completed in 1955 by architect Edward O. Anderson, the enormous structure perched on a small hill is an updated Classical Moderne structure with a gold-leaf statue of the angel Moroni crowning its summit. The '50s also saw the stripped Classical Moderne appearance of Scripps College's Honnold Library, 1952, in Claremont. The design by J.E. Stanton and its 1956 addition by Stanton & Stockwell are crisp enough to appear like the Regency Moderne.

Throughout the 1960s, there were occasional borrowings from the Moderne that ranged from the reserved – as the Pasadena Museum of Art (now Norton Simon Museum), 1969, by Ladd & Kelsey, which drew on the 1930s for its curving corners – to the more blatant neo-Streamline Encino Travelers Insurance Building, 1966, by Howard Lane, on Ventura Boulevard in Encino. In 1969, Art Deco's color and PWA/Classical Moderne's artwork seemed to be the inspiration for Millard Sheets' design of the Home Savings and Loan Association Building at the southeast corner of Wilshire Boulevard and Twenty-sixth Street in Santa Monica. Sheets, an artist, had been a muralist during the WPA-PWA era and his Home Savings architectural design includes mosaics by Nancy Colbath and stained-glass windows by Susan Hertel.

By the early 1970s, Art Deco began to be recognized more widely nationally as a decorative arts and architectural style. There was a conscious analyzation of the elements from all its phases as the style began to be abstracted, conceptualized, and recycled in Post-Modern vocabulary. In Los Angeles, this led to Pomona's Wells Fargo Bank, 1972, as a Classical Moderne revival, and the Streamline Warner Brothers Office Building, 1979, in Burbank, by Charles Luckman Partnership, as well as the Streamline Griger Building, 1972, in Pasadena on Arroyo Parkway, by Daniel, Mann, Johnson and Mendenhall. The 1977 Vista Del Mar Duplex by Eric Owens Moss and James Stafford, with its yellow color and exposed metal flues, appears like a Streamline design influenced by the 1930s Chicago and New York World's Fair buildings of Joseph Urban and Norman Bel Geddes, respectively.

Below:
Adele and the late Ira Yellin preserved the character of the 1929 Dolores Del Rio-Cedric Gibbons house and furnished it with contemporary and imported furnishings that suit the house's Moderne character, as a view of the large second-story living room displays. *Tim Street-Porter*

Opposite page:
In the den of the Del Rio-Gibbons house, the fireplace becomes a part of the abstract-patterned wall which merges with the practical recessed lighting, side table, and built-in sofa. *Tim Street-Porter*

This kind of intelligent recycling of the Moderne styles continued into the 1980s when the Beverly Hills Civic Center was remodeled, 1981-92, by Charles Moore/Urban Innovations and Albert Martin Associates; Campbell and Campbell, landscape architects. Their design is Spanish in flavor, but Art Deco in finish and execution. And in downtown Los Angeles, New York architects Kohn Pedersen Fox picked up on the Post-Modern/Art Deco abstractions in their 1000 Wilshire Building, 1984-87.

The campus of Santa Monica City College features another Daniel, Mann, Johnson, and Mendenhall building that has the suggestion of Streamline Moderne in it: the Business Education and Vocational Building, 1981, which blends it with a version of late International Style. Even sculptor Robert Graham's Doumani House, 1982, in Venice expresses the elegance of the Perpendicular Art Deco Moderne in the vertical treatment of the stucco box, the step-pattern windows, and open-metal grillwork.

Moderne allusions continued to creep into a few designs of the 1990s, such as the Palmetto Construction Headquarters of the Department of Water and Power, 1991-92, by Neil Stanton Palmer Architects (Walter Scott Perry). The white curved metal and Post-Modern green glass walls seem inspired by the Streamline Moderne. Also, the Sony Music Campus, 1992, in Santa Monica, by Steven Ehrlich Architects, is another contemporary design with some curved forms associated with the Streamline mode. And one architect who seemed to purposefully adopt the Moderne for revival in the 1990s is Michael McDonough, whose Bernini House, 1991, on Seventeenth Street

NEW YORK 1930
PARIS 1928-1929
RUHLMANN
RODEO
MARCEL DUCHAMP
AMERICAN ART DECO
CRAFTS
MODERN ART

in Santa Monica has the smooth surfaces, case metal windows, and other signature elements of Art Deco.

Los Angeles' Moderne heritage was appreciated and protected in the late 1970s, the 1980s, and the 1990s, the decades which saw the beginning of the Art Deco Society and the renovations of the Pan-Pacific Auditorium, the Wiltern Theatre, the Oviatt Building, and other such Moderne landmarks. During those decades, the Walt Disney Company also used Art Deco and Streamline icons in its theme parks in Florida and Japan, spurring worldwide enthusiasm for the peculiar Los Angeles structures that evoke a popular progressive spirit.

From the late 1980s to the early 1990s, individuals sought out and bought Moderne houses, like the late real-estate developer Ira Yellin and his wife, Adele, who purchased the Dolores Del Rio-Cedric Gibbons Art Deco house and preserved as much of the original character and features as possible. Another example is singer-actress Barbra Streisand, who created an Art Deco House in Malibu to house her growing collection of Art Deco furnishings. The house was designed to be a simple L-plan pavilion. Without overhangs, but crowned by a stucco cornice of chevrons, the smooth wall surfaces appear crisp and reserved; the stucco-box form of the Streamline era predominates.

The metal-banded staircase set against a window wall becomes a major feature of the first-floor room. *Tim Street-Porter*

Mirror panels, green and black marble, and tube lights create a rich composition in the master bath of the Del Rio-Gibbons house. *Tim Street-Porter*

In the 1970s, Barbra Streisand assembled an Art Deco collection and had a guest house renovated with Art Deco flourishes to accommodate the pieces. Today, the Art Deco-style guesthouse – without the furnishings – can be visited as part of the Ramirez Canyon Park. *© 2001 Renee M. Hadar, All Rights Reserved*

An outdoor sculpture set in the lush vegetation once graced the setting of the Art Deco guest house – designed like a set of linked pavilions defined by an L-planned pool with terraces on two of its sides. *© 2001 Renee M. Hadar, All Rights Reserved*

Without overhangs but crowned by a chevron-patterned stucco cornice, the smooth wall surfaces of the Art Deco guesthouse appear crisp and reserved. Two sides of the pavilion-like guest house are finished in burgundy tile. The color scheme of the exterior – and interiors – was limited to burgundy and gray. © *2001 Renee M. Hadar, All Rights Reserved*

A stepped, semi-circular bench forms the low wall of the Jacuzzi. © *2001 Renee M. Hadar, All Rights Reserved*

One tile wall adjacent to the Jacuzzi is an Art Deco composition: a rectangle flanked by decorative sconces made as the background for a tall black vase.

An outdoor fireplace was made into an Art Deco composition with a curved backdrop and stepped chimney. *© 2001 Renee M. Hadar, All Rights Reserved*

A curved bar and vividly-patterned wallpaper define the entertainment area of the guesthouse. *© 2001 Renee M. Hadar, All Rights Reserved*

A metal-and-glass stair railing decorates the living room staircase leading to the second floor of the Art Deco guesthouse. *© 2001 Renee M. Hadar, All Rights Reserved*

The dining area is located informally adjacent to the kitchen of the guesthouse. Furnishings here once included French upholstered chairs and a black glazed-top table. The tile "rug" remains as a part of the Art Deco guesthouse. *© 2001 Renee M. Hadar, All Rights Reserved*

An Art Deco mosaic and sconces decorated one burgundy wall of the dining area.
© 2001 Renee M. Hadar, All Rights Reserved

One casual seating arrangement in the guesthouse was made up of a French sofa and matching ottomans set against Art Deco wallpaper and patterned rug.

One guest bedroom featured a plush French swan chair and angled layers of diaphanous curtains. © *2001 Renee M. Hadar, All Rights Reserved*

Currently, there are other collectors who have assembled fine collections of Art Deco and Moderne furnishings, housing them in architectural settings that are made appropriate to the works. They bring us full circle to the 1920s *avant-garde* enthusiasm of the Oviatts and Winnetts, who traveled to Paris for the exposition and brought back ideas and quality furnishings that were not being produced locally for their stores – The Oviatt and Bullocks Wilshire.

One such collector is Jules Haimovitz, a television executive, who worked with interior designer Carolyn M. Lawrence and French arts dealer Anne Hauck to create one of the finest collections of imported Art Deco furnishings in Los Angeles. The interior architecture of the Haimovitz residence has been designed to create a fine Art Deco setting with high ceilings, linear mouldings, and stone floors. Lawrence designed certain pieces to complement the high quality French work and she gave the house a contemporary feeling with suitable draperies, rugs, carpets, and other furnishings.

Interior designer Carolyn M. Lawrence and Anne Hauck, owner of Los Angeles' Anne Hauck Art Deco, brought together a formidable collection of Art Deco pieces for the home of television executive Jules Haimovitz. The high-ceilinged entrance area features Art Deco banding to accentuate the ceiling and doorways. The contemporary French pedestal, right, is "Filibustre" Espresso Lacquer by Christian Liagre. French four-panel lacquer screen dates from 1925. The French alabaster and bronze pendant light – one of a pair – is signed by Cheuret, 1925. *Gene Ogami*

A banded cornice defines the dark-hued living room walls. *Gene Ogami*

The Haimovitz library is wood paneled in a classical Moderne manner. It features four amboyna wood Paris Press Club armchairs, 1930-32; an octagonal French side table, circa 1930; and a desk and built-in banquette designed by Carolyn M. Lawrence and built by Nolan Arnold Furniture. *Gene Ogami*

Art Deco furnishings in the living room include: Neo-Art Deco French pieces – "Lambi" sofas, "Mandarin" side chairs and "Cordovan" bench – by Christian Liagre; French Art Deco pieces – leather armchairs designed by Michael Dufet for Jacques Adnet, 1930; a pair of oval Macassar ebony coffee tables, signed Primavera, Paris, 1929; and a pair of 1925 two-tiered oval ebony coffee tables. The artworks are lithographs by Jean Cocteau. *Gene Ogami*

In the new millennium, Los Angeles' furniture makers, designers, and architects have both the rich history of the European movements and the regional talent to draw on. One firm that has taken a highly innovative, playful view of local history is *kwid*, founded by Kelly Wearstler. In completing works as whole design packages – exteriors, interiors, and landscaping – the firm has recycled images form Los Angeles' recent history and given a contemporary feel to the ornament and styles of the past. In particular, they have expanded on the Regency Moderne idiom in their Viceroy Hotel in Santa Monica and the Estrella Hotel & Spa in Palm Springs.

Equally, the preservation and partial renovation of the Sunset Tower, now The Argyle Hotel, has brought a fresh examination of the Art Deco luxury of the past, and has restored to L.A. a sense of style that once again has definite commercial appeal and displays the advertising worth of good design.

Opposite page:
The black paneled powder room features an Erté-style lamp beside the basin. *Gene Ogami*

In the Haimovitz hallway, Moderne detailing is visible in the window framing, and the inset wall shape and moulding. *Gene Ogami*

The architectural structure and wall insets are emphasized in the Moderne-styled master bedroom where French 1930s armchairs and a 1930 Macassar ebony coffee table form a grouping by the window view. The French 1920 sconces are by Leleu; sofa designed by Carolyn M. Lawrence; bed designed by Dakota Jackson. *Gene Ogami*

Jules Haimovitz' collection of vintage clocks from 1920s and '30s France are displayed in an ebony cabinet in the living room. The clock in the upper right is the winner of the Design Award of 1937; it is made of galalite, crystal, and chrome and is signed by Ato. *Gene Ogam*

In Streamline Moderne renovations and preservations, residential work currently predominates. This accounts for individual enthusiasts' rediscovery of the 1930s and '40s William Kesling houses. In addition, the 1930s Elliott House by Rudolph Schindler, and in Palm Springs, the 1930s Ship of the Desert house by Adrian Wilson and Erle Webster and the 1946 residence of industrial designer Raymond Loewy have been restored. These last three residences were the projects of architects Leo Marmol and Ron Radziner, who also reproduce a line of furniture by Rudolph Schindler. Known for their contemporary work and their quality of craftsmanship, Marmol Radziner and Associates is a unique design-build firm that, to date, has been called upon to restore three Neutra houses, several Schindler houses, and Frank Lloyd Wright's 1923 Millard House.

On The Influence of Stylistic Sources and Capitalism

During the 1920s, the American Art Deco style derived from the 1925 Paris Exposition Internationale des Arts Décoratifs et Industriels Modernes and its many examples – from the pure Modern of Le Corbusier to the styles of Hoffmann and others who blended a stripped Classicism with the decorative and craft traditions that remained from the Art Nouveau. Both pure examples and diluted versions of the French style influenced countless architects, designers, and, especially, their clients via various popular and professional publications. Stylishness and ornament were necessary elements of their Art Deco skyscrapers as dramatically represented in Los Angeles, for example, by the 1928 Richfield Building, the 1927-28 Oviatt Building, and the 1928-29 Bullocks Wilshire, and much of the commercial architecture that served the city's car-driven, family-centered consumerist culture.

During the 1930s, the shift to the American Streamline style was derived partly from the body of Art Deco images plus the impact of the European International Style and the many works inspired by Mendelsohn's commercial style to produce pure and diluted versions of the Streamlined box. With the Depression, architects had to make more out of less. In Los Angeles and the region, the Streamline especially thrived with new building types as drive-ins, cinemas, and convenience stores, as well as a great flourishing of apartments and houses. Like temporary fair buildings, the works employed inexpensive means to make broad and bold modern statements as visible in Los Angeles' 1938 Pan-Pacific Auditorium, the 1934-35 Carl's Drive-in, and the 1936 Mauritania Apartments. The style further enhanced the city's consumerist culture.

Since the early twentieth century, the many aforementioned international exhibitions, associations, and publications reflected the intense cultural contacts that provided foreign style guides for a fairly new city in a relatively new country. Even the titles of American books, such as the 1930 *The New World Architecture* (written by a Los Angeles transplant, Sheldon Cheney), promised an American share in the Modern Movement. The 1932 Museum of Modern Art exhibition and the mid-1930s publication of Pevsner's *Pioneers of the Modern Movement* showed a logical certainty and a guaranteed mainstream development by following the lead of the European *avant-garde* architects.

The rapid dissemination of the new architectural styles and their imitations created difficulties for some American modernists because they were committed to the concepts and theories of the European Modern Movement while many of their colleagues were not. For the majority, issues of functionalism, machine symbolism, beauty versus utility, and form versus content were of little importance in America as it recovered from World War I, suffered through the Great Depression, and faced World War II. In fact, in America, overt expression, decoration, and symbolism were appreciated for positive values, and the images of formalist works, such as those by Mendelsohn, Perret, Mallet-Stevens, and Hoffmann, were preferred, since a Modern Movement design was a stylistic choice and traditional habits of ornament and expression were natural in an era in which clients preferred period styles to modern designs and architects needed to guarantee their clients' financial viability.

The 1946 Palm Springs house of industrial designer Raymond Loewy was designed by Albert Frey and shows the evolution of the Streamline style to early post-War modernism. The restoration of the house was completed by Leo Marmol and Ron Radziner. *David Glomb*

A pergola extends out from the Raymond Loewy House. *David Glomb*

The entrance of the 1946 Loewy House. *David Glomb*

The pool flows into the interior of the Loewy House. *David Glomb*

Los Angeles' Art Deco '20s and Streamline '30s and '40s reflected the same interests of the Art Nouveau architects and Viennese Secessionists who, nearly a half-century before, sought new forms to express a new industrially-produced architecture. And much of the work relates to the geometry, clarity, and structural coherence that could be expressed through machine-made materials and technical processes that, to this day, still reflect social and scientific progress. Like those early European Modern movements, the Los Angeles Moderne styles did not end traditional ornament – as Loos had proposed early in the century – but asserted formal representations of technical and industrial processes.

However, the body of L.A.'s Moderne work makes relevant America's interest in the early twentieth-century *avant-garde* culture that continued from Art Nouveau innovations to develop the Modern Movement's functional and methodological architectural expressions, most of which came from the Bauhaus, where architects from various countries unified to seek a rational architecture. While 1930s America did not have the political changes and conflict between democracy and dictatorship of Europe, it had participated in World War I and was well aware of the political difficulties. Additionally, architects were sensitive to the totalitarian visions proposed by the dictatorships' rigid images of arches and columns, as well as their rejection of modernist experiments. American architects followed the development of the Congres Internationaux d'Architecture Moderne (CIAM) and the international movement in architecture to build a better society, especially after 1933, when Bauhaus teachers fled to England and America, and many settled in, or visited, Los Angeles.

To most historians and critics, the Moderne equals capitalism. L.A.'s many émigrés put a damper on the conscience of the Moderne with the parallel rise of Modern Movement architecture in the works of Gill, Wright, Neutra, and Schindler. During the decades in which it flourished, the ideology of an elite modernism was at odds with the ideology of a pseudo-machine style – the utopian land of sunshine and promise compromised into a dystopia of capitalism. The *noir* interpretation persisted into the 1970s.

Rather than the belief that the Art Deco-Streamline architects took a lackadaisical middle course between the High Art Moderns and the Traditionalists, as David Gebhard proposed in his "About Style, Not Ideology" essay, it seems that Moderne architects consciously chose the formal representation of technical and industrial process for the practical purpose of a beneficial capitalist society.

This positive spin on Moderne's decorative styles is fortified by recognizing the many industrial designers intimately involved with technical and structural details who became the heroes of the Moderne. They tended toward a mechanistic approach by their understanding of the workings and structural aesthetics of product design, and applied that understanding as a discipline to interiors and furnishings, as well as to architecture and city planning.

In hindsight, no dystopia manifested itself in Los Angeles and the societal threat of capitalism and advertising did not become the menace to values that the émigrés so believed. The narrow constraints of architectural theories have fallen by the wayside as contemporary culture recognizes the strength of American innovation and ingenuity in the rich complexities of architectural expression.

Los Angeles enjoyed the flashy, crowd-pleasing styles of the Art Deco towers and Streamline slabs and boxes while period-style eclecticism began to fade and European émigré architects who had settled in the city were beginning to recognize the forces of a country where real experiment and discussion could impact European Modern Movement concepts. The Great Depression's spread of the Moderne through federal projects changed conditions in America more than imported ideas of design. It locked in a pragmatic, mechanistic dependence on economy, progress and the advertising value of architecture so aptly reflected in L.A.'s Deco and Streamline works.

Exterior curtains once graced the entrance porch of the original 1942 Pendleton House (now in disrepair), a key example of the Regency Moderne designed by one of its chief proponents John Woolf. *Above*: Recently, the firm called *kwid* have created a neo-Regency Moderne style and the pool area of their design of the Viceroy Hotel in Santa Monica shows an expansion of the Regency Moderne's play of interior-exterior furnishings. *Grey Crawford*

The check-in desk at the Viceroy provides seating and a collage of traditional frames. *Grey Crawford*

The bar at the neo-Regency Moderne Viceroy Hotel. *Grey Crawford*

The living area of a Viceroy Hotel suite. *Grey Crawford*

A bedroom of one of the Viceroy Hotel suites. *Grey Crawford*

The Estrella Hotel & Spa in Palm Springs designed by *kwid* also uses outdoor curtains for its pool and sunbathing pavilions as well as at the entrances to a number of the bungalow suites. *Grey Crawford*

Symmetry and formality define the neo-Regency Moderne at the Estrella Hotel but the right choice of materials makes the pavilions quite comfortable and inviting. *Grey Crawford*

A high-ceilinged bungalow suite at the Estrella Hotel. *Grey Crawford*

Opposite page:
The Estrella's black and white color scheme is accented with colorful details, sculpture, and furnishings that create elegant silhouettes. *Grey Crawford*

Classical Regency style urns and sculpture in one of the Estrella Inn's suites. *Grey Crawford*

Endnotes

1. In popular culture, both the French terms "Moderne" and "Art Deco" were used directly following the opening of the 1925 Exposition Internationale des Arts Décoratifs et Industriels Modernes in Paris, the World Fair that displayed a broad range of modern examples in architecture, interior design, and industrial design, and that influenced numerous American adaptations and offshoots. The term "Art Deco" came into academic usage after a 1966 exhibition, "Les Annees '25' Art Deco/Bauhaus/Stijl/Esprit Nouveau," at the Musée des Arts Décoratifs, Paris. It was then adopted in 1968 by British historian Bevis Hillier to describe a style of design and architecture prevalent in Western Europe and America from the 1920s through the 1930s.

2. David Gebhard and Robert Winter, *A Guide to Architecture in Los Angeles & Southern California*, Santa Barbara: Peregrine Smith, Inc., 1977, p. 702.

3. *Ibid.*

4. Cited in Leonardo Benevolo, *History of Modern Architecture*. Cambridge, Mass.: The M.I.T. Press, 1971, p. 276.

5. Nikolaus Pevsner, *Pioneers of the Modern Movement from William Morris to Walter Gropius*, London: Pelican Books, 1936, p. 114.

6. Benevolo, *op. cit.*, p. 330.

7. Cited in Luther Munz, *Adolf Loos*, Milan: Electa Books, 1956, p. 13.

8. Munz, *op. cit.*, p. 27.

9. Richard Neutra, *Survival Through Design*, Oxford: University Press, 1954, p. 300.

10. Benevolo, *op. cit.*, p. 301.

11. *Ibid.*, p. 549.

12. Cited in Christian Norberg-Schulz, *Meaning in Western Architecture*, New York: Praeger Publishers, 1975, p. 366.

13. Norman Bel Geddes, *Contempora Exposition of Art and Industry*, New York Art Center, 1929.

14. "Frank Lloyd Wright and Hugh Ferris Discuss This Modern Architecture," *Architectural Forum*, 53:536, November 1930.

15. Sheldon Cheney, *The New World Architecture*, New York: Tudor Publishing Co., 1930, p. 82.

16. Aldous Huxley, "Puritanism in Art," *Creative Art*, 6:201-202, March 1930.

17. Patricia Bayer, *Art Deco Architecture*, London: Thames & Hudson, 1992, p. 8.

18. Mike Davis, *City of Quartz, Excavating the Future in Los Angeles*, New York: Verso, 1990, p. 19.

19. *Ibid.*, p. 48.

20. Cited in Davis, *op. cit.*, p. 49.

21. David Gebhard, preface from Patrick Pascal, *Kesling Modern Structures*, Los Angeles: Balcony Press, 2002, p. 9.

22. Rudolph Schindler, "Modern Architecture: A Program," 1912, cited in August Sarnitz, *R.M. Schindler*, New York: Rizzoli, 1988, p. 42.

23. Sheldon Cheney, *Art and the Machine*, New York: McGraw-Hill Book Co., 1936, p. 166-68.

24. This survey brings together some similar categories of buildings within Moderne's phases and may include some demolished works or structures that have been extensively remodeled.

Resources

Antique Malls

The Antique Alley
706 State Street
Santa Barbara, California 93101
Tel: 805-962-3944

Antiques & More
327 Pine Avenue
Long Beach, California 90802
Tel: 562-437-3040

The Antique Guild
3225 & 3231 Helms Avenue
Los Angeles, California 90034
Tel: 310-838-3131; Fax: 310-838-2934
www.theantiqueguild.com

Antiques on Fair Oaks
330 South Fair Oaks Avenue
Pasadena, California 91105
Tel: 626-229-9590; Fax: 626-449-9441

Cannery Row Antique Mall
471 Wave Street
Monterey, California 93040
Tel: 831-655-0264; Fax: 831-655-0265
www.antiqnet.com/canneryrow

Dusty Old Things
431 East Broadway
Long Beach, California 90034
Tel: 562-938-1158

Elan Collection
2218 East Fourth Street
Long Beach, California 90814
Tel: 562-434-1895

State Street Antique Mall
710 State Street
Santa Barbara, California 93101
Tel: 805-964-3795

Antique Shows

Bustamante Antique Shows
Tel: 209-358-3134
www.bustamante-shows.com

Great America Collective
1736 Lombard Street
San Francisco, California 94123
Tel: 415-922-2650

L.A. Modernism Show
Santa Monica Auditorium
www.caskeylees.com

Long Beach Outdoor Antique & Collectible Market
Long Beach Veterans Stadium
6200 East Conant Street
Long Beach, California 90808
www.longbeachantiquemarket.com

The Pasadena Antique Center & Annex
440 & 480 South Fair Oaks Avenue
Pasadena, California 91105
Tel: 626-449-7706

R.G. Canning's Rose Bowl Flea Market
(2nd Sunday each month)
1 Rose Bowl Drive
Pasadena, California 91103
Tel: 323-560-7469
www.rgcshows.com

Santa Monica Antique Market
1607 Lincoln Boulevard
Santa Monica, California 90404
Tel: 310-314-4899

Auctions

A.N. Abell Auctioneers & Appraisers
2613 Yates Avenue
Commerce, California 90040
Tel: 323-724-8102
www.abell.com

Bonham & Butterfield Auctioneers & Appraisers
7601 West Sunset Boulevard
Los Angeles, California 90069
Tel: 323-850-7500

www.Christies.com
www.Sothebys.com

Antiques & Accessories

Anne Hauck
8738 Melrose Avenue
Los Angeles, California 90069
Tel: 310-659-3606; Fax: 310-659-3678
www.annehauckartdeco.com

Big City Galleries
Malibu, California 90265
Tel: 310-457-9282

Blackman-Cruz
800 North La Cienega Boulevard
Los Angeles, California 90069
Tel: 310-657-9228

Deco Deluxe
993 Lexington Avenue
New York, New York 10021
Tel: 212-472-7222

Delorenzo
956 Madison Avenue
New York, New York 10021
Tel: 212-249-7575; Fax: 212-861-7507

Doris Leslie Blau
15 East 57th Street
New York, New York 10021
Tel: 212-586-5511

First 1/2
P.O. Box 5030
Palm Springs, California 92263
Tel: 760-322-1160

Harry
8639 Venice Boulevard
Los Angeles, California 90034
Tel: 310-559-7863

Macklowe Gallery & Modernism
667 Madison Avenue
New York, New York 10021
Tel: 212-644-6400; Fax: 212-755-6143

Marvin Alexander
315 East 62nd Street
New York, New York 10021
Tel: 212-838-2320; Fax: 212-754-0173

Myers-Huffman
8663 Nash Drive
Los Angeles, California 90046
Tel: 323-656-9789

Newel Art Galleries
425 East 53rd Street
New York, New York 10022
Tel: 212-758-1970; Fax: 212-371-0166
www.newel.com

Thanks For The Memories
8319 Melrose Avenue
Los Angeles, California 90069
Tel: 323-852-9407

Watch Me Tick
191 South Beverly Drive
Beverly Hills, California 90212
Tel: 310-278-8458

X21
890 Valencia Street
San Francisco, California 94110
Tel: 415-647-4211; Fax: 415-695-0797
www.x21modern.com

Antique Reproductions

Jean De Merry
225 North Robertson Boulevard
Los Angeles, California 90069
Tel: 310-205-0991; Fax: 310-205-0993
www.jeandemerry.com

Historic Lighting
114 East Lemon Avenue
Monrovia, California 91016
Tel: 626-303-4899; Fax: 626-358-6159

Shapes Collection
10201 National Boulevard
Los Angeles, California 90034
Tel: 310-839-7400; Fax: 310-839-7500
www.shapescollection.com

Architectural Restoration/Renovation

kwid
317 South Kings Road
Los Angeles, California 90048
Tel: 323-951-7151; Fax: 323-951-7455

Brenda Levin and Associates
811 West Seventh Street, Suite 300
Los Angeles, California 90017
Tel: 213-623-8141; Fax: 213-623-9207

M2A Milofsky and Michali Architects
6253 Hollywood Boulevard, Suite 210
Los Angeles, California 90028
Tel: 323-464-0600; Fax: 323-464-0615
m2a@m2a-architects.com

Marmol and Radziner Architecture & Construction
2902 Nebraska Avenue
Santa Monica, California 90404
Tel: 310-264-1814; Fax: 310-264-1817

Architectural Salvage

Architectural Detail
512 South Fair Oaks Avenue
Pasadena, California 91105
Tel: 626-844-6670

Architectural Salvage of San Diego
1971 India Street, Suite 114
San Diego, California 92101
Tel: 619-696-1313

Tony's
123 North Olive
Orange, California 92866
Tel: 714-538-1900; Fax: 714-938-1966

Urban Archaeology
285 Lafayette Street
New York, New York 10012
Tel: 212-431-6969

Tile

Ann Sacks
8483 Melrose Avenue
Los Angeles, California 90069
Tel: 323-658-8884; Fax: 323-658-8842

California Art Tile
8687 Melrose Avenue
West Hollywood, California 90069
Tel: 310-659-2614

Textiles

Textile Artifacts
12589 Crenshaw Boulevard
Hawthorne, California 90250
Tel: 310-676-2424; Fax: 310-676-2242
www.textileguy.com
www.archiveedition.com

Online Shopping Services

www.artdeco.com
www.circline.com
www.ebay.com

Bibliography

Applebaum, Stanley. *The New York World's Fair 1939/1940.* New York: Dover Publications, 1977.

Battersby, Martin. *The Decorative Twenties.* New York: Walker & Company, 1969.

Battersby, Martin. *The Decorative Thirties.* New York: Walker & Company, 1971.

Bayer, Patricia. *Art Deco Architecture.* London: Thames & Hudson, 1992.

Bayer, Patricia. *Art Deco Interiors.* London: Thames & Hudson, 1990.

Bel Geddes, Norman. *Contempora Exposition of Art and Industry.* New York: Art Center, 1929.

Benevolo, Leonardo. *History of Modern Architecture.* Cambridge, Massachusetts: The M.I.T. Press, 1971.

Bogardus, Emory Stephen. *Southern California, A Center of Culture.* Los Angeles: USC Press, 1938.

Breeze, Carla. *L.A. Deco.* New York: Rizzoli, 1991.

Bush, Donald J. *The Streamlined Decade.* New York: George Braziller, 1975.

Chapman, John L. *Incredible Los Angeles.* New York: Harper and Row, 1967.

Cheney, Sheldon. *Art and the Machine.* New York: McGraw-Hill Book Co., 1936.

Cheney, Sheldon. *The New World Architecture.* New York: Tudor Publishing Co., 1930.

Davis, Mike. *City of Quartz, Excavating the Future in Los Angeles.* New York: Random House, 1992.

Duncan, Alastair. *American Art Deco.* New York and London: Abrams, 1986.

Ferris, Hugh. *The Metropolis of Tomorrow.* New York: 1929.

Frankl, Paul T. *Form and Re-Form.* New York: Harper & Bros., 1930.

Frankl, Paul T. "Modern Will Live." *California Arts and Architecture* 53 (1933): 17-19.

Frankl, Paul T. *New Dimensions, The Decorative Arts of Today in Words and Pictures.* New York: Payson & Clarke, Ltd., 1928.

Gebhard, David. "L.A. – Stuccoed Box." *Art in America* 58 (1970): 130-133.

Gebhard, David and Von Bretton, Harriette. *Kem Weber: The Moderne in Southern California, 1920-1941* (exhibition catalog). Santa Barbara: University of California, 1969.

Gebhard, David and Von Bretton, Harriette. *L.A. in the Thirties, 1931-1941.* Salt Lake City: Peregrine Smith, Inc., 1975.

Gebhard, David and Winter, Robert. *A Guide to Architecture in Los Angeles & Southern California.* Santa Barbara: Peregrine Smith, Inc., 1977.

Gibling, Pauline. "Modern California Architects." *Creative Art*, Vol. 10 (February 1932): 111-115.

Grief, Martin. *Depression Modern: The Thirties Style in America.* New York: Universe Books, 1975.

Hanks, David. *Innovative Furniture in America from 1800 to the Present Day.* New York: Horizon Press, 1981.

Heide, Robert and Gilman, John. *Popular Art Deco, Depression Era Style and Design.* New York: Abbeville Press, 1991.

Hillier, Bevis. *Art Deco of the 20s and 30s.* London: Studio Vista, 1968.

Hillier, Bevis. *The World of Art Deco* (exhibition catalog). New York: Dutton, 1971.

Hitchcock, Henry-Russell. "An Eastern Critic Looks at Western Architecture." *California Arts and Architecture* 57 (1940): 21-23, 40.

Hitchcock, Henry-Russell and Johnson, Philip. *The International Style: Architecture Since 1922.* New York: Museum of Modern Art, 1932.

Longstreth, Richard. *The Drive-In, The Supermarket and the Transformation of Commercial Space in Los Angeles, 1914-1941.* Cambridge: The MIT Press, 1997.

McCoy, Esther. "Roots of California Contemporary Architecture." *Arts and Architecture* 73 (1956): 14-17.

McCoy, Esther. "Wilshire Boulevard." *Western Architecture and Engineer* 222 (1961): 24-31.

McWilliams, Carey. *Southern California: An Island on the Land.* Salt Lake City: Peregrine Smith, Inc., 1983.

McWilliams, Carey. *Southern California Country.* 1946. Reprint, Salt Lake City: Peregrine Smith, Inc., 1973.

Meikle, Jeffrey L. *Twentieth Century Limited: Industrial Design in America 1925-1939.* Philadelphia: Temple University Press, 1979.

Mock, Elizabeth, ed. *Built in USA, 1932-1944.* New York: Museum of Modern Art, 1944.

Neutra, Richard. *Survival Through Design.* Oxford: University Press, 1954.

Pascal, Patrick. *Kesling Modern Structures.* Los Angeles: Balcony Press, 2002.

Pevsner, Nikolaus. *Pioneers of Modern Design from William Morris to Walter Gropius.* New York: Museum of Modern Art, 1949.

Pildas, Ave. *Art Deco Los Angeles.* New York: Harper & Row, 1977.

Pilgrim, Dianne. *The Machine Age in America 1918-1941* (exhibition catalog). Brooklyn: Harry N. Abrams, 1986.

Poulos, Arthur J. *American Design Ethic: A History of Industrial Design to 1940.* Cambridge: The MIT Press, 1983.

Powell, Lawrence Clark. *Land of Fiction*. Los Angeles: Dawson's Book Shop, 1952.

Robinson, Cervin and Bletter, Rosemarie Haag. *Skyscraper Architecture: Art Deco New York.* New York: Oxford University Press, 1985.

Scarlett, Frank and Townley, Marjorie. *Arts Décoratifs 1925: A Personal Recollection of the Paris Exhibition.* London: Academy Editions, 1975.

Schindler, Pauline, guest editor. "Special Issue Devoted to Modern Architecture in Southern California." *California Arts and Architecture* 47 (January 1935).

Shivers, Natalie and others. *L.A.'s Early Modernism: Art Architecture Photography.* Los Angeles: Balcony Press, 2003

Starr, Kevin. *Endangered Dreams: The Great Depression in California.* New York: Oxford University Press, 1996.

Starr, Kevin. *Material Dreams: Southern California Through the 1920s.* New York: Oxford University Press, 1990.

Taylor, John Russell. *Strangers in Paradise, The Hollywood Emigres 1933-1950.* London: Faber and Faber, 1985.

Teague, Walter Dorwin. *Design This Day, The Technique of Order in the Machine Age.* New York: Harcourt Brace & Co., 1940.

Valentine, Maggie. *The Show Starts on the Sidewalk.* New Haven: Yale University Press, 1994.

Varian, Elayne H. *American Art Deco Architecture* (exhibition catalog). New York: Finch College Museum of Art, 1974.

Weaver, John D. *El Pueblo Grande.* Los Angeles: Ward Ritchie Press, 1973.

Weber, Eva. *Art Deco in America.* New York: Exeter Books, 1985.

Weiss, Peg. *The Art Deco Environment.* Syracuse: Everson Museum of Art, 1976.